RIVERS of the WORLD

The Rio Grande

RIVERS
∿ *of the* ∿
WORLD

The Rio Grande

Titles in the Rivers of the World series include:

The Amazon
The Colorado
The Congo
The Ganges
The Mississippi
The Nile
The Rhine
The Rio Grande
The Yangzte

RIVERS
~ of the ~
WORLD

The Rio Grande

James Barter

**LUCENT
BOOKS®**

THOMSON
GALE

San Diego • Detroit • New York • San Francisco • Cleveland • New Haven, Conn. • Waterville, Maine • London • Munich

LIBRARY OF CONGRESS CATALOGING-IN-PUBLICATION DATA

Barter, James, 1946-
  The Rio Grande / by James Barter.
    p. cm. — (Rivers of the world)
Summary: Details the geologic features of America's second longest river, describes
the human communities, ecosystems, and wildlife habitats in or near the river, and
examines the causes of the current depletion of the water and efforts to restore
this natural resource.
Includes bibliographical references and index.
  ISBN 1-59018-365-7
  1. Rio Grande—Juvenile literature. 2. Rio Grande Valley—Juvenile literature. [1. Rio
Grande. 2. Rio Grande Valley. 3. Rivers.] I. Title. II. Rivers of the world (Lucent Books)
  F392.R5B37 2003
  976.4'4—dc21

                                                    2003003540

Contents

• • • • • • • • • • • • •

Foreword

· · · · · · · · · · · · ·

Human history and rivers are inextricably intertwined. Of all the geologic wonders of nature, none has played a more central and continuous role in the history of civilization than rivers. Fanning out across every major landmass except the Antarctic, all great rivers wove an arterial network that played a pivotal role in the inception of early civilizations and in the evolution of today's modern nation-states.

More than ten thousand years ago, when nomadic tribes first began to settle into small, stable communities, they discovered the benefits of cultivating crops and domesticating animals. These incipient civilizations developed a dependence on continuous flows of water to nourish and sustain their communities and food supplies. As small agrarian towns began to dot the Asian and African continents, the importance of rivers escalated as sources of community drinking water, as places for washing clothes, for sewage removal, for food, and as means of transportation. One by one, great riparian civilizations evolved whose collective fame is revered today, including ancient Mesopotamia, between the Tigris and Euphrates Rivers; Egypt, along the Nile; India, along the Ganges and Indus Rivers; and China, along the Yangtze. Later, for the same reasons, early civilizations in the Americas gravitated to the major rivers of the New World such as the Amazon, Mississippi, and Colorado.

For thousands of years, these rivers admirably fulfilled their role in nature's cycle of birth, death, and renewal. The waters also supported the rise of nations and their expanding populations. As hundreds and then thousands of cities sprang up along major rivers, today's modern nations emerged and discovered modern uses for the rivers. With more mouths to feed than ever before, great irrigation canals supplied by river water fanned out across the landscape, transforming parched land into mile upon mile of fertile cropland. Engineers developed the mathematics needed to throw great concrete dams across rivers to control occasional flooding and to store trillions of gallons of water to irrigate crops during the hot summer months. When the great age of electricity arrived, engineers added to the demands placed on rivers by using their cascading water to drive huge hydroelectric turbines to light and heat homes and skyscrapers in urban settings. Rivers also played a major role in the development of modern factories as sources of water for processing a variety of commercial goods and as a convenient place to discharge various types of refuse.

For a time, civilizations and rivers functioned in harmony. Such a benign relationship, however, was not destined to last. At the end of the twentieth century, scientists confirmed the opinions of environmentalists: The viability of all major rivers of the world was threatened. Urban populations could no longer drink the fetid water, masses of fish were dying from chemical toxins, and microorganisms critical to the food chain were disappearing along with the fish species at the top of the chain. The great hydroelectric dams had altered the natural flow of rivers, blocking migratory fish routes. As the twenty-first century unfolds, all who have contributed to spoiling the rivers are now in agreement that immediate steps must be taken to heal the rivers if their partnership with civilization is to continue.

Each volume in the Lucent Rivers of the World series tells the unique and fascinating story of a great river and its people. The significance of rivers to civilizations is emphasized to highlight both their historical role and the present situation. Each volume illustrates the idiosyncrasies of one great river in terms of its physical attributes, the plants and animals that depend on it, its role in ancient and modern cultures, how it served the needs of the people, the misuse of the river, and steps now being taken to remedy its problems.

Introduction
∙∙∙∙∙∙∙∙∙∙∙∙∙∙∙∙∙∙∙

The River That Can No Longer Find Its Way to the Sea

The Rio Grande is a river that has lost its way. Following what geologists estimate to be more than a million years of wending its way from the high alpine elevations of the Rocky Mountains, through the hot, arid climate of the Southwest, and finally to the Gulf of Mexico, this great river can no longer find its way to the sea.

As the Rio Grande, a Spanish name meaning "Great River," courses through the desert lands of America's Southwest, its immense volume of water at the outset gradually dwindles and dies before reaching the gulf. Despite its critical value to all residents along its path, this great river is in a state of crisis, and many scientists and environmentalists fear it may be nearing the point of complete collapse.

People divert water from the river's flow for a variety of reasons. Most of the river is allocated to irrigate millions of acres of cropland, some goes to process manufactured goods in factories, and the remainder to quench thirsty mouths and gardens in millions of homes and dozens of burgeoning cities from Colorado through New Mexico and Texas. Hydrologists, scientists who study the characteristics of freshwater bodies such as rivers, lakes, and underground water sources called aquifers, assert that "claims to the Rio Grande's flow exceed the actual supply. Inefficient irrigation systems continue to drain most of the river's water." [1]

Water is undoubtedly the Southwest's most precious natural resource, not only in the United States but in Mexico as well. Both countries share water from the Rio Grande, called the Río Bravo del Norte in Mexico, meaning the "Wild River of the North." The river and its tributaries that lie deep within each country are heavily depleted to support agriculture, cities, factories, generation of hydroelectricity, and river recreation. Today, sections of dry riverbed are signs that this region is undergoing rapid population growth and a diminishing water supply.

People, however, are not the sole cause for the depletion of the river's water. Hydrologists report that nature takes its share as well. Evaporation causes billions of gallons to disappear during the hot summer season. Droughts also take their toll, as do river blockages caused by growths of

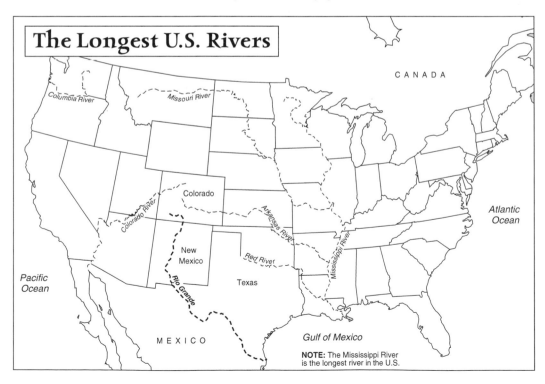

The Longest U.S. Rivers

Columbia River

Missouri River

CANADA

Colorado

Colorado River

Arkansas River

Mississippi River

New Mexico

Red River

Atlantic Ocean

Pacific Ocean

Rio Grande

Texas

MEXICO

Gulf of Mexico

NOTE: The Mississippi River is the longest river in the U.S.

The Rio Grande supplies the American Southwest and Mexico with water. The river also supports a number of ecosystems and wildlife habitats.

aquatic vegetation. Between people's needs and nature's unpredictability, the Rio Grande struggles more than ever to reach the sea.

The great river, however, is not merely the lifeblood of human communities in the Southwest. It is also the biological backbone for ecosystems and wildlife habitats found throughout this arid landscape. Eighty percent of all vertebrate species in the Southwest depend on riparian, or

riverbank, areas for at least part of their life cycles, and over half of these species cannot survive without regular access to them. As the river's volume is depleted, the wildlife is the first to suffer.

Environmentalists are not optimistic about the Rio Grande's future. "In general, it's a dying river," [2] said Susan George, attorney for Defenders of Wildlife in the city of Albuquerque, New Mexico. She continued, "The lack of flows to sustain aquatic creatures and the lack of flooding to preserve the bosque [an area with thick river vegetation] point to an ecosystem in decline." [3] Mary Lou Campbell, conservation chairwoman of the Sierra Club chapter in the Rio Grande Valley, adds, "It's a disaster in the making." [4] Campbell notes that there has already been a major fish kill near Brownsville, Texas.

Such pessimism is borne out by hydrologists, who have tracked the declining flow of the river. The flow has stopped entirely some years, as one report indicates: "The average annual flow rate at the mouth of the Rio Grande before 1962 was just under 3 million cubic meters [3.9 million cubic yards]. The 1990–1995 average was 0." [5]

Restoring the Rio Grande and its smaller tributaries, which function as the ribbons of life in this desert ecosystem, has captured the attention of civic as well as government leaders. All recognize that the river is the most important natural resource for preserving the region's biological heritage as well as everyone's way of life. Forest Guardians, a nonprofit conservation organization working with the University of Texas to restore the Rio Grande basin, takes the position that "unless action is taken today to reverse the impending collapse, we may lose more than just a few endangered species." [6]

As the twenty-first century moves forward, all concerned users of the river's water agree that this great struggling river needs immediate assistance in the form of sweeping changes in the way it is used. Scientists are working to make changes along the river that will benefit both agriculture and riparian wildlife. Lawyers also play a role by renegotiating and rewriting water agreements drawn up early in the twentieth century that no longer address the needs of all users living within the river basin. Shifting population concentrations and changing water-use patterns demand compromises to help the Rio Grande once again find its way to the sea so all who have benefited from its waters can continue to benefit.

1

• • • • • • • • • •

A Desiccated River

The Rio Grande is America's second longest river, North America's fourth longest, and the twenty-fourth longest in the world. From its origins high in the Rocky Mountains of southern Colorado, it travels nineteen hundred miles while dropping nearly two and a half miles in elevation. In the course of dropping to sea level, the river darts south through the heart of New Mexico and slants southeast to form the international boundary with Mexico as it passes through Texas before emptying into the Gulf of Mexico at Brownsville. Despite the river's name, which suggests size and power, for fifteen hundred miles of this run to the sea, the river swelters and shrivels to a mere trickle in the intense heat of one of America's hottest and most desolate regions.

The Rio Grande Basin

The area of the Rio Grande basin, sometimes also called the catchment, is defined by three distinct geological features, according to geographers and hydrologists. The first is the Rio Grande itself and all of its tributaries; the second is the

The Rio Grande is America's second longest river. From its source in the Rocky Mountains, the river travels nineteen hundred miles before emptying into the Gulf of Mexico.

floodplain, which comprises those areas parallel to the banks of the river that are flooded during rare occurrences of heavy rains; and the third is all of the mountains and plains that drain into the Rio Grande and its tributaries. This total area is estimated to be 335,000 square miles, 180,000 of which are in the United States and 155,000 in Mexico.

The Rio Grande is the source of life for about 13 million Americans, as well as wildlife living in the basin. The river and its tributaries traverse the American states of Colorado, New Mexico, and Texas and the Mexican states of Durango, Chihuahua, Coahuila, Nuevo León, and Tamaulipas. As the river moves along, only a handful of tributaries from Mexico and the United States, such as the Conchos, Pecos, and San Juan Rivers, ensure permanent flow because the river loses as much water to evaporation as it acquires from its tributaries.

The Rio Grande is the only American river to define a lengthy international border. From El Paso to the Gulf of Mexico, roughly 1,250 miles, the Rio Grande's basin is divided between the United States and Mexico. Both countries share the basin's water. How the river is used on each side of the international border affects water flowing to the other side. The river also creates a shared cultural barrier. El Paso, Texas, to the Gulf, and Ciudad Juárez, Chihuahua, for example, make up the largest of seven pairs of twin cities that straddle the river along the border. The river has also been in the midst of political and economic struggles between the two countries for more than two hundred years and even one war.

A tractor plows through floodwaters in a section of the Rio Grande floodplain. Flooding is a common occurrence along the Rio Grande.

Geologists divide the river's trek into three distinct regions of uneven lengths: the upper, middle, and lower. In this way, they are able to make reference to distinct geologic and climatic features as well as changes in the variety of wildlife species.

The Upper Rio Grande

The Rio Grande arises as a trickle from melting snow high in the San Juan Mountains of southern Colorado. This climatic zone, 12,500 feet above sea level, is classified by geographers as either alpine or sometimes arctic-alpine. Winter gales drop as much as fifty feet of snow when biting temperatures drop as low as sixty degrees below zero, Fahrenheit. If there is not substantial snowpack each winter, which accounts for half of the total volume of the river, the needed water for the Rio Grande will not be available. This thick winter blanket of snow rejuvenates this great river each year when the spring and summer sun warms the peaks to release the first pristine drops of water.

The San Juan Mountains are one segment of the much larger Rocky Mountains range that runs on a north-south axis through Colorado. As snow melts and trickles down the eastern side of the San Juan range, it gradually gains speed and volume, rushing through pine-covered mountainsides into the broad and lush San Luis Valley basin.

The river continues flowing due east through some of Colorado's gold- and silver-mining towns. First passing through Creede, Wagon Wheel Gap, and South Fork, the river then flows into Alamosa, about 125 miles from its start. At this point, it takes an abrupt turn south. Along its eastward run, the Rio Grande gains in strength by the addition of dozens of small tributaries. Here, it cascades through several gorges and its elevation plummets forty-five hundred feet before departing Alamosa for New Mexico.

The dash to Alamosa is one of the most picturesque segments of the Rio Grande. The rapid drop in elevation results from the scouring, or carving action, of the river as it slices its way through the San Juan Mountains. Scouring occurs when the fast-moving river rubs against the bottom and sides of the mountains, dislodging millions of tons of alluvium, a mixture of sand, silt, gravel, and dirt. Over much of this 125-mile dash, the river careens through several deep gorges with mountain walls towering thousands of feet above. These mountains, peppered with tall pines, remain snowcapped until late into the warm summer months.

Departing Alamosa, the Rio Grande heads due south fifty miles, cascading into white-water turbulences as it crosses into New Mexico. From the border it flows through high-desert elevations, passing the cities of Taos and Espanola, where the tributary the Rio Chama joins the main flow, and then through White Rock, until slowing down and settling into the city of Albuquerque at fifty-three hundred feet above sea level.

There, the river departs high mountains and narrow gorges to broaden out on fairly level land. At the end of this first stretch, it has only traveled 325 miles, just 17 percent of its total distance, but it has already completed more than half of its total drop in elevation to sea level. The remainder of the journey will be hot and slow.

The Middle Rio Grande

Albuquerque sits on a broad, flat plateau, slowing the rush of water and allowing the river to broaden and soak the desert. From Albuquerque to the end of the middle segment, at the city of Truth or Consequences, New Mexico, the river traverses its shortest segment of only 130 miles.

As the river departs Albuquerque, it continues due south, passing through the cities of Los Lunas, Belen, Socorro, and finally Truth or Consequences. This hot, arid region is part of the Chihuahuan Desert, one of the driest ecosystems in America, typically receiving less than six inches of annual rainfall. Although there are a few tributaries along this stretch of river, the majority are dry washes most of the year unless an occasional flash flood occurs following a rare thunderstorm.

A yucca plant blooms along the middle Rio Grande. Due to the hot temperatures in this section of the river, billions of gallons of water evaporate each year.

The desiccated nature of this region means that the Rio Grande receives little, if any, additional volume from its tributaries. This segment of the river is further impacted by a severe loss of water from evaporation as it flows across the desert. Intensely hot desert temperatures, which remain above 100 degrees Fahrenheit without relief between late May and October, translate into a loss of billions of gallons of water to evaporation. This condition, coupled with the inability of tributaries to contribute to the Rio Grande's

volume, means that in the space of just 130 miles, far more water departs Albuquerque than arrives at the end of the middle section of Truth or Consequences. From there, the river flows into Elephant Butte Reservoir, 455 miles from its source.

The Lower Rio Grande

The lower Rio Grande begins as its water cascades over the largest dam on the river, Elephant Butte Dam. From here, the river travels two hundred miles south to the city of El Paso, which sits just across the border from New Mexico. When the river crosses into Texas, it defines the border between the United States and Mexico for the remainder of its route to its outfall into the Gulf of Mexico at the city of Brownsville. This last and longest segment of the Rio Grande, 1,250 miles, is more than three times the length of the combined lengths of the upper and middle segments.

As the Rio Grande departs El Paso, its route turns to a southeast direction for the next 325 miles until it encounters a sudden turn, channeling the water abruptly north. This 118-mile bend in the river, aptly named Big Bend, is the result of volcanic and seismic activity buckling the earth and uplifting the Chisos Mountains. Compelled to follow canyons deep within these mountains, the river bends north, funneling through a series of three spectacular narrow canyons, Santa Elena, Mariscal, and Boquillas, which form the southern Big Bend National Park boundary. As the river threads its way through these deep canyons, steep vertical walls tower fifteen hundred feet above.

Immediately before the Rio Grande reaches Big Bend, and then again after departing it, the river replenishes its dwindling volume of water. First, it receives the flow of its tributary the Conchos River from deep within Mexico at its confluence at the city of Presidio. After departing Big Bend on its northern path, it is again refreshed at the city of Langtry by the waters of the Pecos River flowing through Texas. At this point, the Rio Grande renews its southeast direction toward the sea.

From Langtry, the river meanders through the desolate Texas hill country until reaching the cities of Laredo and Zapata, where the Salado River tributary joins the Rio Grande. During its long run from Elephant Butte Dam, the elevation of the river gradually drops so that roughly one hundred miles before the river pours into the Gulf of Mexico, its elevation is only thirty feet above sea level. At this point, the Rio Grande has slowed down, causing it to gradually break out from its narrow bed and fan out across the landscape, creating the delta region.

The delta, a wetland area in the shape of a triangle, is occasionally saturated by the broadening Rio Grande. By the time the river reaches its outfall at the gulf, it has inundated fifty miles of land on each side. The delta's apex is positioned roughly one hundred miles inland from the coast, and its arc of shoreline is about one hundred miles long, creating a total delta area of five thousand square miles; twenty-four hundred square miles of delta are in the United States, and the remaining twenty-six hundred are across the border in Mexico.

Over the course of millions of years, the Rio Grande has deposited millions of tons of alluvium throughout the delta, creating a wetland environment rich in nutrients. Brian Tapley, who studies and maps the delta using satellite photographs, makes the point that

> prior to the construction of dams, floodways, and levees along its course, the Rio Grande typically overflowed its banks annually, depositing new sediment and sending water into a variety of discharge meander channels [canals created by floods] . . . in the delta. These flood waters constituted significant [nutrient-rich] freshwater input into the marshes of the Rio Grande Delta.[7]

Geology

Geologic activity that shaped the North American continent many millions of years ago explains why the Rio

The Conchos River

The Conchos River is the largest of the Rio Grande tributaries with an average annual flow of over 265 billion gallons of water, one-third of which belongs by treaty to the United States. Its basin is one of the most important river systems in all of northern Mexico. From its headwaters high in the Sierra Madre Occidental at an elevation of seventy-two hundred feet, to its banks bordered by large irrigation districts in the central plains of the state of Chihuahua, to its confluence with the Rio Grande just above Big Bend National Park, the Conchos River is an essential ribbon of life in an arid desert climate. The Conchos River basin covers about 26,400 square miles, roughly 14 percent of the total area of the Rio Grande basin.

Within the Conchos River basin, Mexico has constructed seven dams on the river, five of which are operated primarily for water storage. These dams can store large volumes of water, especially when the river experiences high peak flows of as much as seventy-one thousand cubic feet per second. Stored water is later released during the hot summer season to irrigate fields of corn, alfalfa, winter wheat, pecans, melons, and a variety of small vegetables. Ninety percent of all stored water is used for crop irrigation, and the remaining 10 percent goes to cities, the eight largest of which support a total population of about 1.1 million people. The other two of the seven dams provide both water storage and hydroelectricity.

The governmental agency overseeing Mexico's water supply, Comisión Nacional de Aguas (CNA), has raised grave concerns about the river's water quality. The CNA has made the claim that the Conchos River has been converted into Mexico's biggest collection system of contaminated agricultural and municipal wastewater. Runoff carrying pesticides and animal waste from farms, combined with the direct discharge of raw human sewage from hundreds of cities and villages, threatens the health of everyone dependent on the river for their drinking water.

Grande begins its journey high in the San Juan Mountains of southern Colorado, why it abruptly cascades down through New Mexico, and why it continues across the searing hot deserts of Texas until plunging into the sea at the Gulf of Mexico.

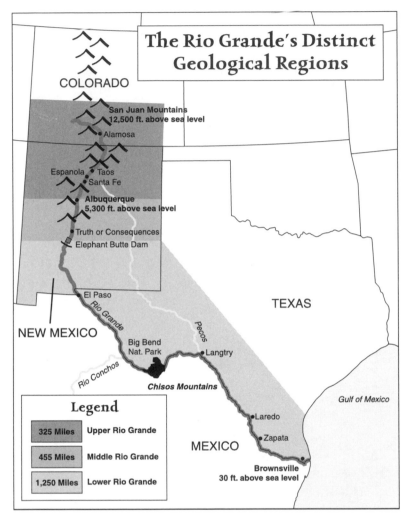

The Rio Grande's Distinct Geological Regions

COLORADO

San Juan Mountains
12,500 ft. above sea level

• Alamosa

Espanola • Taos
• Santa Fe

Albuquerque
5,300 ft. above sea level

• Truth or Consequences
Elephant Butte Dam

El Paso •

Rio Grande

NEW MEXICO

TEXAS

Big Bend
Nat. Park

Pecos

• Langtry

Rio Conchos

Chisos Mountains

Gulf of Mexico

• Laredo

• Zapata

MEXICO

Brownsville
30 ft. above sea level

Legend

325 Miles	Upper Rio Grande
455 Miles	Middle Rio Grande
1,250 Miles	Lower Rio Grande

Geologists explain that 20 million years ago the portion of the earth's crust called the North American geologic plate collided and scraped along the eastern edge of the Pacific plate just off the coast of California. The pressure resulted in an uplift, also called up-warp, that created the Rocky Mountains and several other smaller mountain ranges. Parts of Colorado and adjacent states rose five thousand feet above the undisturbed plains below.

During this time of uplift, a second significant activity occurred. The earth's stretched and brittle crust formed a series of rifts, sometimes also called troughs or valleys. This long chain of closed rifts, each isolated from the others, formed a chain of small lakes from Colorado south into Mexico. Over another several million years, intense volcanic activity caused large amounts of sand, gravel, lava, and volcanic ash to fill these many rifts. Finally, they combined into one long, continuous rift that is today named the Rio Grande rift, which runs southward through Colorado and New Mexico into the Mexican state of Chihuahua.

As the rifts combined, so did their lakes, one cascading into the next. Eventually, the dozens of isolated lakes formed

The River and the Moose

With the exception of fish and a few amphibians, the moose of the upper Rio Grande is better adapted to live in and around the river than any other species. The largest of all animals along the upper river, bulls weigh in at sixteen hundred pounds while cows peak at eleven hundred pounds. Standing seven feet at the antlers, this remarkable species is built to spend its entire life either in the water or very close to it.

Unlike its cousins the deer, the antelope, and the elk, a moose must stay connected to the river for survival. Its enormous weight requires it to consume food in the form of grasses at the rate of between forty and fifty pounds a day. Such a high volume of vegetation forces the moose to seek out tall and thick grasses that can only grow in the river and throughout its floodplain.

The unusual claw-shaped antlers on the moose are designed to help it forage for food. With its fifty-inch antler spread, the moose can be seen wading into the river and completely submerging its head down to the riverbed, where it drags its antlers to rip up and trap vegetation. After exiting the river, the moose shakes off the mat of plant life and devours it.

The moose is also one of the few big grazing animals confident about swimming long distances in the river. Its enlarged hoofs, which act as paddles, combined with its ungainly long legs, allow the big animal to plunge into the river and swim to escape predators such as wolves or to cross rivers to find more favorable grazing lands. Swimming provides two secondary benefits: It relieves much of the animal's enormous weight from its spindly legs, and it also acts as a cooling system to lower the animal's body temperature during the summer's heat.

the flowing Rio Grande. As snowmelt continued to cascade down the new mountains formed by the up-warp activity, the Rio Grande rift finally channeled it to the sea.

Fauna

The geology of the Rio Grande basin also played a major role in the types of animals that now inhabit the river basin. The dramatic changes of elevation between the upper and lower sections of the river create climatic variations that leave a permanent covering of snow on the highest Colorado mountain peaks while scorching the New Mexico desert sands. Such geologic and climatic differences determine the animal life capable of surviving within the Rio Grande's diverse habitats.

Near the headwaters of the upper river, the dominant animals that depend on the river's water include many of the largest in North America. Of all the fauna of the Rio Grande basin, the brown bear is the most imposing and dominant. Weighing up to six hundred pounds, bears prefer grasslands and lowland wooded areas close to rivers and streams large enough to provide them with a plentiful supply of fish, their principal source of protein. Bears are masters at catching fish. They wade out into streams and, with lightning quick flicks of their large paws, either impale a fish or flip it onto the riverbank for easy eating. In these cold, high-elevation waters, bears favor six species of trout, walleye, both smallmouth and largemouth bass, humpback chub, and razorback sucker.

The high elevation is also the home of many of North America's largest grazing mammals. Bighorn sheep, famous for their curled horns; sixteen-hundred-pound moose; deer; elk; and antelope populations live here. Many of these herbivores obtain moisture from vegetation during the cool seasons but are forced to the rivers to drink and forage during the summer.

Far from Colorado, near the border of New Mexico and Texas, the desert environment is home to an array of animals very different from those in Colorado. This desiccated and hot region, where summer temperatures peak at 120 degrees Fahrenheit, is the domain of a dazzling array of reptiles, which includes dozens of sand-burrowing lizards and snakes such as the poisonous sidewinder rattlesnake. The sidewinder takes its name from its sideway motion, which gives it the traction needed to traverse loose sand.

One of the more fascinating reptiles is the Gila monster, not a monster at all but rather one of America's largest lizards. Known to have scales that look like tiny red, yellow, and black beads, this lizard is sometimes called a beaded lizard. With a stout body that grows two feet long, the Gila monster survives in the desert climate by eating small mammals, birds, and eggs. When threatened, it may flatten its body, crawl into a tight fissure in a rock, and then bloat its body with air, making it almost impossible to extract. If attacked, however, the Gila monster is capable of delivering a mildly poisonous bite that will kill or stun other small animals.

Brown bears are frequent visitors to the Rio Grande basin, where these large animals can find fish.

Flora

Rio Grande basin flora, like the fauna, changes dramatically within the three river regions. In the upper river, the alpine ecosystem (above eleven thousand feet) and the subalpine ecosystem (between nine thousand and eleven thousand feet), both small plants and large trees must survive hurricane-force winds, arctic temperatures, and an extremely short growing season. To adapt, alpine plants form ground-hugging, mosslike clumps with long taproots. Many tundra plants have dense hairs on stems and leaves to buffer the wind or red pigments that convert sunlight into heat and screen out high doses of ultraviolet radiation.

The large trees, such as Engelmann spruce, ponderosa pine, Douglas fir, and lodgepole pine, thrive and occasionally grow up to two hundred feet during their one-thousand-year lifespan. Alpine conifers are adapted to the strong winds and frigid temperatures atop the high peaks. The branches of the spruce and fir trees are short and brittle, so they tend to grow close together to buffer the wind; both of these species have narrow, pointed crowns, which help shed snow. In contrast, the subalpine pines have more open crowns with flexible branches, which help them withstand heavy snowfalls and blustery winds with less damage.

Far from the alpine snows and rains, along the middle and lower river basin, rainfall plummets dramatically to four to six inches annually. Plants there have adapted to the dry, hot climate by altering their physical structures in one of three primary ways. Those that conserve water by reducing transpiration, the loss of moisture to the hot air, are called xerophytes. Xerophytes, such as cacti, usually have special means of storing and conserving water. They often have few leaves, and many species have had their leaves evolve over millions of years into spines that do not allow transpiration at all.

The second principal group, the phreatophytes, comprises plants that have adapted to arid environments by growing extremely long roots, allowing them to acquire moisture at or near the water table. These plants are able to produce modified leaves because they have a supply of water deep underground. Most of the phreatophytes are various species of grasses.

The last desert group, the ephemerals, survives by remaining in a dormant state until heavy rains trigger it to bloom. The most colorful and beautiful of the entire desert flora, ephemerals, such as poppies, blossom into vibrant purples, yellows, reds, and blues. Sometimes ephemerals may remain in their dormant state for years awaiting soaking spring rains, but generally they bloom once a year. The blooming season is short, and the plants must germinate quickly or the seeds for the next season will never be ready for the rains.

2

· · · · · · · · · ·

The Ancient Ones

To a greater extent than any other force of nature, the Rio Grande River determined the lifestyle of those inhabiting its banks. Early natives living along this nineteen-hundred-mile-long Rio Grande basin depended on the river, directly or indirectly, as the provider of their foods, medicines, transportation, and spiritual inspiration.

Archaeologists who have carried out excavations of early dwellings, primarily in New Mexico and Texas, have evidence to support the theory that the earliest inhabitants arrived about fifteen thousand years ago, when the last ice age first began to subside. These early tribes, called Paleo-Indians (*paleo* from a Greek word meaning "old"), spread out over the entire American Southwest. At this time one major tribe, known as the Anasazi, a Navajo word meaning "Ancient Ones," flourished side by side with several smaller tribes, such as the Hohokan, Hopi, and Zuni.

Much of what archaeologists know about the Paleo-Indians comes from petroglyphs, more commonly known as rock paintings. Archaeologist Reed McManus describes the West Mesa Escarpment monument that borders the Rio Grande:

Along the 17 miles of winding cliff face known as the West Mesa Escarpment, predecessors of modern Pueblo Indians etched thousands of petroglyphs between 1000 B.C. and A.D. 1650. The images depict religious life: headdresses, masks, the flute player Kokopelli, meandering rivers, macaws, mountain lions, horned serpents, human figures, bears, and sun symbols. Elsewhere in the monument are the ruins of a 1,000-room pueblo, hundreds of archaeological sites, and the five volcanic cones that produced the vast, inspiring canvas for early rock artists. [8]

Initially the Anasazi hunted wild animals for food and clothing. They pursued woolly mammoths, giant bison, wolves, and saber-toothed tigers using weapons made of bone and stone. Then, about ten thousand years ago, as the climate throughout North America warmed further, the glaciers began melting and the large, ferocious ice-age

Paleo-Indians lived along the river and left their mark in the form of petroglyphs, like these at Albuquerque's Petroglyph National Monument.

animals became extinct. Without these huge animals, the Paleo-Indians slowly adapted to hunting smaller animals and invented spears and bows and arrows to hunt them. Some of the people began to subsist on aquatic animals and learned to weave nets to catch fish while supplementing their diets with roots, berries, nuts, fruits, and grass seeds.

About five thousand years ago, agriculture began when tribes along the lower Rio Grande began to plant corn. The development of agriculture meant that the Indians could maintain a more stable food source and food supplies, and they could have more leisure time to settle down and develop more complex communities, called pueblos. Archaeological evidence reveals that the stretch of river most densely inhabited by early tribes was within the warmer regions along the middle and lower river. Excavations there have unearthed the remains of charred foods, proving that corn, squash, and beans were major crops. The location of many of these excavation sites, within a mile of the Rio Grande or one of its tributaries, is also evidence of the importance of the river in the lives of the natives.

As the early Indians settled down, growing reliable crops each year became increasingly important. Grains and vegetables not only provided a well-balanced meal when combined with wild game, but they also made the Indians less dependent on hunting. To ensure bountiful crops, Indian tribes learned to farm with the assistance of the Rio Grande.

Early Agriculture

The Anasazi culture gradually evolved from being dependent on hunting to a dependence on agriculture. Most lived close to the river in pueblos tucked into canyon walls and canyon valleys, but by A.D. 1300 the Anasazi mysteriously vanished. Archaeologists studying the Indians of the Southwest believe that a terrible twenty-five-year-long drought forced them to move away. Their descendants are the Pueblo Indians of the Rio Grande Valley of New Mexico.

First to Cultivate Corn

Corn was a critical staple to early American Indians in the Southwest, and it remains one of the few major indigenous crops widely eaten by modern Americans. Although some disagreement exists among agro-anthropologists—anthropologists who study the foods of early peoples, most studies generally agree on the date corn was first cultivated but not necessarily the first tribes to do this.

The two most widely accepted places for the earliest cultivation of corn are northern Colorado and southern New Mexico. Both regions contain evidence for early cultivation from perhaps as far back as 500 B.C. until about A.D. 1500. Native Americans of both regions developed a lifestyle that allowed them to successfully cultivate and store corn.

Indian farmers planted, irrigated, harvested, and stored corn in small granaries. Storage of corn was not only for later eating but also for later use as seed when the climatic conditions were right to plant the next crop. Anthropologists theorize that Indians could predict the coming season by studying wildflowers. Prehistoric farmers knew when to plant based on when these flowers bloomed.

Not all anthropologists, however, agree that corn was first cultivated by two tribes living in different locations. In July 1999 R.G. Mason, writing for *Southwestern Archaeology* magazine, proposed that the earliest evidence for maize cultivation in the Greater Southwest would be found not with the Fremont in northern Colorado but rather in the lowland floodplains of southern Arizona and New Mexico. He further believes that the earliest dates are much earlier that those associated with the Fremont.

Mason believes that the cultivation of corn began in Mexico as far back as 3500 B.C. and that the technique eventually migrated north into the southwestern United States. Samples of corn from regions in the southern parts of the Southwest date to 1700 B.C. In *Southwestern Archaeology* magazine, Mason further contends: "One would expect the earliest maize-based villages to be found not on the Colorado Plateau, but in the Basin and Range Province to the south. I also reasoned that the Anasazi tradition, and thus the Pueblo peoples, might be the end result of such a process."

Living in the Southwest desert, the Pueblo tribes learned that growing crops would require irrigation. Although some winter rains could be expected to wet the parched earth, most would be reclaimed by the scorching summer heat.

In order to wet the roots of basic crops, desert dwellers devised an early system of irrigation ditches called *acequias,* a Spanish word meaning "irrigation canals."

The Pueblo Indians were reported to have been practicing irrigation farming when the Spanish explorers and colonists first came to the region during the mid–sixteenth century. One Spanish explorer who entered New Mexico in 1583 reported finding "many irrigated corn fields with canals and dams, built as if by the Spaniards." [9] At the Acoma Pueblo, a small village in New Mexico, the same explorer noted, "These people have their fields two leagues [six miles] distant from the pueblo, near a medium-sized river, and irrigate their farms by little streams of water diverted from a marsh near the river." [10]

The evidence of the acequias can still be found throughout the middle and lower parts of the Rio Grande. These irrigation ditches were typically one to three feet deep and two to five feet wide. They were built up against the banks of the nearest river and carried water as far as two miles inland. The corn, bean, and squash crops were then irrigated by smaller lateral irrigation ditches that distributed water from the acequias to the roots of the crops. Since the Indians did not cultivate their fields with plows, it was not necessary to plant their crops in straight rows to provide space for plows to unearth weeds. Instead, the plants were scattered equidistant from one another about the fields.

Dams were also part of the irrigation system. Pueblo Indians constructed low-lying, compacted earthen dams called check dams. Archaeologists have discovered evidence for check dams, rarely more than three feet tall. The dams consisted of a series of stone walls built straight across very small streams. Initially the check dams confined the water, causing it to seep deep into the ground to root systems. Over time, each check dam created a small, fertile crop area behind it as moist sediment built up, allowing for prime growing conditions.

In addition to corn, beans, and squash, Rio Grande basin Indians harvested several plants native to the area, such as a variety of wild seeds, mesquite beans, and many different roots. Several types of cacti were eaten, such as the prickly pear and the saguaro, both of which produced a fruit that the Indians mashed, boiled in water, and made into jam.

One of the most utilitarian plants irrigated and harvested was an agave called yucca. This plant was the most useful because its long fibers could be used to make baskets, ropes, fishing nets, and sandals, and its roots were ground to make a kind of soap. Archaeologists have also found evidence in fire pits of roasted chunks of the softer tissue of the yucca, which were eaten.

With the exception of the water, no characteristic of the river was more important to early Indians than the fish that lived in it. For tribes living within the hot, desolate regions of the middle and lower river basin, where large game animals were scarce, fish was the primary source of protein, and fishing was their secondary occupation after farming. For these reasons, early fishermen devised many different ways to catch their meals.

Fishing

The importance of fish in the lives of tribes along the Rio Grande is underscored by evidence revealing many different fishing techniques and equipment. The Indians utilized a wide variety of fishing equipment to catch different fish from different riverine environments. Unlike the fishermen of other great rivers, Rio Grande natives apparently did not fish from canoes, preferring instead to fish from the riverbank, while wading in the water, or from platforms built in calm streams. In addition to a variety of fishing locations, they also had various fishing techniques. Archaeological evidence, both actual fishing artifacts as well as petroglyphs, indicate the use of nets, lines and hooks, spears, weirs, and even the use of poisons. Three of the more interesting techniques involved the net, weir, and poison.

Evidence of nets, primarily derived from petroglyphs, indicates two different types: the seine and the dip net. Both nets were apparently made of the long fibers of the yucca, although some archaeologists believe that the Anasazi and the Pueblo tribes also wove them, like baskets, from wicker and thin strips of animal skins.

The seine was a long, narrow net stretched across a small creek or held by two people at each end in a larger river. The technique for snaring fish was a three-step process: First, fishermen extended the seine until it obstructed several fish, then they wrapped it around the fish, and finally they drew it tight, trapping the fish in the middle. Although many escaped, if the seine was closed slowly, without startling the fish, those in the middle could be flung onto the bank.

The dip net was a saucer-shaped wicker basket, about six or seven feet in diameter, attached to a pole by a long rope. Indians lowered the basket two or three feet under the water and waited for a fish to swim into it or just above it. With a quick upward jerk of the pole, the attached basket snatched the fish out of the water. To perform this technique skillfully, Indians built small platforms on poles anchored in still waters several feet from shore.

All early peoples on all major rivers throughout the world used the weir, a fencelike structure designed to trap and impound fish on a river. The tribes throughout the Rio Grande basin typically built them out of materials such as sticks or woven wicker mats. The principle was to barricade a small stream with the weir, allowing water to pass through but not fish. As fish became trapped on one side of the weir, the Indians used their dip nets to pluck them from the water.

The use of the weir and nets, which captured the fish uninjured, meant that live fish could be stored for later consumption. Archaeologists at the University of New Mexico have identified dwelling sites with large pits several feet deep containing fish skeletons along with many one-inch-long J-shaped artifacts that appear to have been stone fishhooks. According to archaeologist David Roberts in his book *In Search of the Old Ones: Exploring the Anasazi World of the Southwest,* "It is quite reasonable to assume that fish may have been stocked in the pits that functioned as fish ponds."[11]

The natives understood that bows and arrows and spears could also be used to catch fish, but not as efficiently as poisoning stream water. Fish poisoning was most effective in still or slow-moving water where fish were concentrated. Native groups in the Rio Grande basin used poisonous plants, such as buckeye or soaproot, to kill small fish. These two plants were cut and beaten with rocks until their poisonous juices were released. Then, with dripping plants in

The River and Cordage

Cordage is the term used to describe the variety of woven items produced by early American Indians using river reeds, grasses, and occasional desert plants such as the yucca. Native Americans have always possessed a vast knowledge of cordage. The basic methods of this ancient technology have remained relatively unchanged. Cordage is made from two or more strips of plant fibers that are twisted or plied together.

Among early Indians within the Rio Grande basin, the long, fibrous river grasses and reeds that flourished in the floodplain provided excellent material for fabricating a dazzling variety of practical products necessary for the functioning of the tribe. Most elaborately designed and ornately painted were woven baskets, made in dozens of designs to suit different storage needs for food and other goods. Following basketry, cordage was widely used to weave sandals, fishing nets and fishing lines, rope, mats, belts, sewing thread, and a variety of decorations.

The first step in manufacturing cordage requires gathering tall river plants, preferably at least four feet long; pounding the stalk; and peeling the desired inner stringy fibers away from the woody part of the stalk. The methods for making rope or heavy cord from fibers involve anchoring two or three lengths of fibers to a post and tightly twisting and weaving each length in turn over and under the others. A simpler and faster method, although not as strong, is called "thigh rolling." The person rolling uses two small bunches of fibers of different length and drapes their ends over his or her thigh; then the person rolls the strands down his or her thigh using the palm of the hand. As the cords roll together, more bundles are added until the desired length is achieved.

hand, the Indians waded into a small, quiet stream and rinsed the poisons into the water. All fish in the immediate downstream area were paralyzed, allowing them to be easily scooped from the water. Failure to remove the fish quickly, however, might cause mild sickness for those who ate the poisoned fish.

Hunting

Fish was not the only source of protein along the Rio Grande. This was particularly true along the upper river, where game was much larger and also more plentiful throughout the year than in the drier regions to the south. The principal advantage of hunting large game rather than fish was the amount of meat provided by one kill. One adult deer could provide enough meat for a tribe of fifty people for one or two days, an elk for three or four days, and a moose could feed a tribe for a week. According to Scott A. Elias, professor of anthropology at the University of Colorado,

> By about 8000 B.C. people of the Archaic [8000–1000 B.C.] culture were utilizing most of the Colorado Plateau. These hunter-gatherers did not settle down in villages, but probably followed the movements of game animals, and gathered food plants through the seasons of the year. [12]

The hunt provided more than food. Of equal importance to the early tribes was the use of animal skins for their winter quarters, blankets, warm clothing, canoe coverings, and shoes. The hides most prized in the colder elevations were those of the moose, elk, deer, and, occasionally down on the plains, buffalo.

Elias and other archaeologists have also concluded that the best place for early Indian tribes to hunt swift-footed animals was near the river, where they could ambush their prey as the animals approached to drink. Archaelogists reached this conclusion for two reasons: First, excavations near riverbanks reveal evidence of hunting weapons along with large caches of animal bones. Elias contends that early tribes hunted with several styles of "projectile points, sharp pointed heads of stone or other material, attached to a shaft to make a projectile that is thrown or shot as a weapon. These include spearheads, arrowheads, and darts."[13] And second, they hunted near the river because hunting big animals in the open ranges without swift horses was extremely difficult. The use of the horse for hunting was not introduced until the arrival of the Spaniards in the fifteenth century.

Tribes in the hot deserts also needed to hunt. Unlike tribes of the upper river however, those farther south became adept at catching small game. A wide assortment of rodents, reptiles, and birds made up part of their diet. Rodents included rabbits, mice, and ground squirrels. Birds such as doves, quails, and roadrunners were also caught. Some tribes also cooked unusual dishes that made use of tortoises, lizards, and snakes.

Catching slow-moving reptiles was an easy proposition, but catching rabbits and other small rodents was another matter. Anthropologists believe that small game was most likely trapped just like fish. They think that the Indians conducted communal rabbit hunts that first required the Indians to dig a deep, long, narrow furrow, wide at one end but narrow at the other, which functioned as a funnel. Next, they stretched a net across the narrow end of the ditch. Then, when the net was in place, the Indians began driving hundreds of rabbits from a wide area into the wide end of the furrow, where they were entangled in the net.

Indians hunted for prey, like this roadrunner, near the water. It was easier to catch animals drinking from the river.

River Travel

The Rio Grande was more to the early inhabitants than a source of food and water. It enabled them to travel more easily. Travel on land within the river basin was slow and difficult before the arrival of the horse. The high elevation and rugged terrain of the upper section made for slow and strenuous hiking, and travel in the middle and a lower sections was especially hot and wearisome during the long summer. Transporting goods was an even more difficult task without horses to pull wagons.

To facilitate passenger and freight travel, all tribes along the river took advantage of its easy flow by traveling down it in various types of canoes and river rafts. All of the earliest explorers of the Rio Grande, from the Spaniard Francisco Vásquez de Coronado in 1540 to many of his successors, made references in their diaries about encountering

Indians navigated the river with canoes made of tree bark or animal skin.

Indians floating down the river in canoes. Their claims are corroborated by petroglyphs depicting canoes and rafts as well as by oral Indian folklore, which has been passed on for many generations in the form of stories and songs. According to Edwin Tappan Adney and Howard I. Chapelle in their book *The Bark Canoes and Skin Boats of North America,* "The canoe was the most commonly built craft and the type of canoe was dictated by the availability of materials." [14] The three most common types of canoes used by early Indians were bark, animal skin, and dugout. Along the upper Rio Grande, where trees and large animals abounded, all three types were used. Farther downriver, however, the dugout canoe was most commonly found.

Bark canoes, as the name implies, were constructed with an outer skin of tree bark, usually from the aspen found in abundance high in the Colorado mountains. Natives peeled the bark of the aspen, which is thin yet durable, into small sheets that were sewn into larger sheets, pleated, and then contoured to a wooden frame with ribs forming the canoe's inner shell. The bark was caulked with tree sap to seal it from water leakage. The techniques of sewing, binding, carving, selecting, and preparing materials were very sophisticated, and designs varied from tribe to tribe. These canoes were lightweight, and when rapids were encountered, travelers simply departed from the river and carried their canoes to calmer waters.

Animal-skin canoes were similar to bark canoes, with the notable exception that the wood frame was covered with animal skins rather than with bark. Skins were larger, more pliable, and water resistant, so these canoes lasted much longer than their bark counterparts. Skins favored were the largest available, usually deer, elk, and moose. But because these hides were also valued for clothing and outer coverings for dwellings, sometimes the skins of smaller but more numerous animals, such as beavers, were sewn together and stretched over the canoe frame. To maintain skin canoes as long as possible, they were always carried from the river to dry as soon as a trip was completed.

The large, heavier canoes, commonly referred to as dugout canoes, were made by felling large trees, letting them sit for several months until they were dry, and then burning the insides out of them—a process requiring careful attention. This rather tricky process first required a general hollowing of the tree to create a furrow most of the length of the tree. The Indians placed tree sap in this furrow and set it on fire. In this way, the tree was hollowed and the resulting coal scraped out with sharp rocks, shells, or animal bones. These dugout canoes, much heavier than the bark or skin canoes, had the advantages of lasting longer and of being able to carry more people.

River Spirits

Tribal dependence on the Rio Grande for sustenance and transportation elevated the river to the status of a religious icon. Anthropologists explain that all river tribes practiced polytheism, the worship of many gods. Many of their cultural beliefs and rituals not only centered on the importance of the river, but they also elevated the river to the status of the gods.

The Rio Grande was perceived as a place of spiritual significance where tribes could go to worship. The Pueblos, for example, considered themselves spiritually connected to the river while worshiping along its banks. Giving thanks to the river was accomplished in a variety of ways, including a river-feeding ceremony during which tribal fishermen returned captured fish to the river to demonstrate their appreciation for the food the river provided them. Another religious ceremony provided tribal members an opportunity to share some important object with the river god by placing the object in the water and watching the river carry it away.

Linda Cordell, a specialist on the heritage of the Pueblo Indians, makes the point that water, including the river, figured in their spiritual beliefs:

The prehistoric Pueblo Indians elaborated themes dealing with water and rain to ensure crops. Cloud blow-

ers (pipes) produced smoke to simulate and attract clouds. Frogs, fish, rivers, and snakes were painted on ceramics and molded from clay. Shrines were often located in the mountains and near springs. The rain cloud motif was painted on seed jars and the walls of kivas [dwellings].[15]

The Rio Grande was respected and appreciated by the early Indians. They viewed the river as the provider of many of their basic needs. Such a poetically simple relationship might have gone on for many more generations had the Spanish and other foreigners not discovered the potential of the river and its basin.

Indian tribes worshiped many gods and viewed the Rio Grande as a spiritual place. Tribes thanked the river for the food it provided with religious ceremonies like this one.

3

....

The Workhorse of
the Southwest

For millions of years before the arrival of the first Indian tribes, the Rio Grande flowed unabated to the sea. Beginning roughly fifteen thousand years ago, the first modest Indian societies made their homes along the river without noticeably impacting either the river or the lands it drained. Even with the arrival of the Spaniards during the mid–sixteenth century, followed by Mexico's three hundred years of supremacy, and then the American conquest during the mid–nineteenth century, little was asked of this great river.

The advent of the twentieth century made a workhorse of the Rio Grande. As America completed its westward movement with a network of railroads fanning out across the Southwest, settlers hoping for a better life moved into the region attracted by open spaces and cheap land. The economies of Colorado, New Mexico, and Texas surged, attracting to this arid landscape still more newcomers hoping to share in the new prosperity. As they poured into these states, demands for water surged for agriculture, cities, industrial use, and recreation. As water freely flowed from the Rio Grande, bubbling across fields, cities, and into homes, this watery backbone became known as "the Workhorse of the Southwest."

The Arrival of the Spanish and Americans

In 1527 explorer Álvar Núñez Cabeza de Vaca departed from Spain as part of a royal expedition intended to occupy the mainland of North America. Following a shipwreck one year later in Florida, he and his men built another boat and sailed west along the coast of the Gulf of Mexico. By 1532, following a second shipwreck, Cabeza de Vaca and his men landed near Galveston and marched through Texas all the way to Arizona. While traveling, Cabeza de Vaca met Indians who told fanciful tales of great wealthy cities farther north. To the Spaniards, this could only mean hoards

Pueblos, like this one in Cliff Palace, Colorado, housed Indian families near the Rio Grande.

of gold and silver. In 1537 Cabeza de Vaca returned to Spain to publish his journal.

Shortly thereafter, in 1539, Francisco Vásquez de Coronado began his expedition to look for the "Seven Cities of Gold" that had been reported by the survivors of Cabeza de Vaca's group. After two years of fruitless exploration, the dispirited Coronado abandoned his search for riches. Nonetheless, Coronado sailed up the Rio Grande, taking careful note of the river, the natural resources, and the native populations. His journals enticed more Spanish to the area, and within a few decades the Spanish colonized the river basin. Cities and church missions began to emerge.

Spanish colonization of Mexico and most of the Rio Grande basin continued for the next three hundred years, during which time Native Americans were forced to convert to Catholicism, to work for the Spaniards, and to relinquish their independence. At the turn of the nineteenth

Francisco Vásquez de Coronado searches the Southwest for the "Seven Cities of Gold." He documented his observations of the Rio Grande in his journals.

century, Mexico revolted against Spain to reclaim all of its lands. Within fifty years, Mexico was embroiled in a war with the United States that concluded in 1848 with the Treaty of Guadalupe Hidalgo. This treaty stipulated the purchase of much of California, Arizona, New Mexico, and Texas from Mexico.

The treaty finally defined America's southern border, much of which follows the contour of the Rio Grande. It played a major role in America's westward movement, eventually paving the way for the railroads and tens of thousands of farmers and ranchers who stampeded into this vast unsettled territory. The Rio Grande went to work as towns sprang up along railroad hubs, ranchers raised cattle, and farmers fenced off their verdant vegetable crops with barbed wire.

Thirsty Crops

Demands for irrigation water started shortly after the first wave of American farmers began tilling the narrow band of fertile land hugging the meandering river. This narrow riparian band, not more than half a mile on either side of the river, was quickly purchased for farming, and subsequent farmers were forced to raise crops farther from the life-sustaining waters.

By the turn of the twentieth century, large-scale mechanized irrigation was introduced into the middle section of the Rio Grande basin, allowing thousands of acres farther from the river to become productive. As the amount and types of crops grew, the railroad was able to transport them throughout the nation. Giant water-pumping stations on the Rio Grande helped to transform the arid landscape of the middle and lower stretches into lush cropland. One such pumping station, built and operated by the Louisiana–Rio Grande Canal Company, went into operation in 1909 to irrigate Texas cropland farther than ten miles from the river. In the city of Hidalgo, the company constructed a large pump house complete with boilers, sixty-inch pumps, engines, and a large smokestack to supply irrigation to forty thousand acres of thirsty crops.

At this same time in New Mexico, even bigger irrigation plans were afoot. A narrow point in the river between the cities of Albuquerque and Las Cruces was designated as the location for the first major diversion on the river. A concrete-and-steel dam was designed to control occasional floods, but, more importantly, it also stored and diverted water to thirsty fields in New Mexico. Construction on the Elephant Butte Dam began in 1907 and was completed in 1916. The dam has a storage volume of 1.3 million acre-feet (AF) of water (one acre-foot being equivalent to 360,000 gallons). Following it in 1936, the Caballo Dam, with a storage capacity of 112,000 AF, was constructed just seventeen miles downriver.

Suddenly awash in water, the deserts of the middle and lower Rio Grande began to bloom. In southern New Mexico, about three-quarters of irrigated land was planted with cotton, alfalfa, and pecans, and the remaining quarter produced chilies, onions, corn, and a variety of other vegetables. In West Texas, cotton, peppers, onions, and pecans sprouted while the hot but more humid climate farther downriver produced thousands of acres of citrus groves.

By 1990 the state of New Mexico boasted 1 million acres of desert crops under irrigation, which proved to be the foundation of the state's economy. The very same year, Texas made a similar claim of irrigating 1 million acres with Rio Grande water, mostly going to its huge citrus groves. For both states, Rio Grande water was clearly the lifeblood of their economies, which employed an estimated eight hundred thousand workers in agriculture.

The significance of Rio Grande water use for agriculture became clear when, in 1993, hydrologist Sherman R. Ellis and his colleagues stated the extraordinary statistic that "89 percent of the Rio Grande River basin's water resources are devoted exclusively to irrigation." [16]

Urban Growth

Urban growth has steadily followed the splash of irrigation water across the Southwest landscape. The flourishing pros-

Elephant Butte Dam

Elephant Butte Dam, completed in 1916 at a cost of $5.2 million, is the largest structure on the Rio Grande. The dam stands 300 feet high while extending 1,675 feet across the river. Containing 618,785 cubic yards of concrete, it was engineered to store about 2.1 million acre-feet of water. Classified by structural engineers as a concrete gravity dam, this large concrete hulk creates a massive downward gravitational push of roughly 1.08 million tons pressing down into the desert floor and sealing the river's water behind the dam in New Mexico's largest lake.

Construction began in 1912, and work was completed in 1916. There was an extensive infrastructure constructed onsite that included railroads, water tanks, material warehouses, and a large construction community complete with tent housing, cafeterias, a hospital, and recreation facilities. Both American and Mexican workers lived in the temporary camps, where the population ranged between eighteen hundred and thirty-five hundred people throughout the construction. At the time of its completion, the dam was the largest structure built in the United States to impound water, creating the world's largest man-made reservoir.

In 1937 Elephant Butte Dam was retrofitted with hydroelectric generators capable of producing twenty-eight thousand kilowatts of electricity. Service is provided over a 490-mile electrical grid assisted by eleven substations.

The highest storage ever recorded at Elephant Butte Reservoir was 2,302,800 AF, which was two feet above the spillway crest, on June 16, 1942. The lowest storage at the dam occurred on October 15, 2001, when the reservoir volume shrank to only 907,300 AF during a drought year.

perity readily seen in the drenched pecan, onion, pepper, and citrus groves, triggered an equally impressive spurt in urban growth. The more water that was channeled to crops ever farther from the river, the more workers poured into the Rio Grande River basin looking for steady employment to plant, irrigate, fertilize, pick, process, and ship the river's bounty. They found the work they were looking for and in the process also found favorable communities for their families.

Today's major cities along the nine-hundred-mile-long Rio Grande were small, dusty, western cow towns 150 years

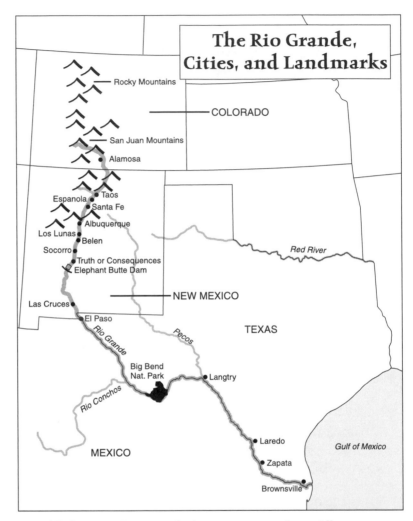

The Rio Grande, Cities, and Landmarks

ago. Today's major population centers, such as Albuquerque, Las Cruces, El Paso, Del Rio, Laredo, and Brownsville, were better known in the distant past for cattle stampedes down Main Street and lawlessness that provided a wealth of stories, mostly fanciful, of western gunslingers, saloons, gambling halls, and legendary heroes who fought to tame the West.

Today these same modern cities are gifts of the Rio Grande. Their population trends reflect the harnessing of the big river; and Albuquerque serves as a good example. In 1860, before any major diversions of the Rio Grande's water, the city's population was 1,760. By 1900 the population was 7,515, and following some major irrigation projects, the population doubled by 1920 to 15,000. As dams and irrigation ditches were built, causing agriculture to boom, the population skyrocketed to 96,000 in 1950, then again to 243,000 in 1970. Today the population stands at 450,000, with an estimated population of 550,000 by the year 2010. This same trend is also true for El Paso, which experienced an increase from 10,000 to 650,000 residents between 1880 and 2000. Laredo's population increased from 3,811 to 200,000 over the same period.

The Urbanization of the Southwest

Roughly around 1950, as the demographic statistics indicate, a population explosion began along the length of the Rio Grande that continues to this day. Although agriculture was the initial economic engine of the basin's economy, the dry climate, combined with the picturesque open spaces and inexpensive living, eventually attracted hundreds of new industries over the next several decades. Of greatest impact on the basin were industries such as aerospace, military installations, health care, clothing and chemical manufacturing, and computer technology. In order to attract these industries, which could further propel the region's prosperity, cities followed the model of urban growth that had first been designed and implemented by southern California cities.

To compete with southern California for industry and people, cities along the Rio Grande followed the Los Angeles model of spreading out rather than up; cities built tracts of homes and shopping centers across the landscape, far from downtown businesses. And unlike homeowners prior to the 1950s, the new householders luxuriated in air conditioning, landscaped yards controlled by automatic sprinkler systems, and swimming pools in as many backyards as possible.

Cities also luxuriated. Urban developers, eager to attract more people, designed golf courses scattered throughout the metropolitan landscapes. City planners designed parks beautified and cooled by shade trees and grass athletic fields for little league and soccer players. Shopping malls followed with expansive landscaping, waterfalls, and air-conditioned stores that attracted sweltering shoppers.

With a basin population increasing at unprecedented rates, growing cities were forced to demand more of the Rio Grande than they had in the past. Cities drew off more water to satisfy urban demand as they grew and prospered side by side with agriculture. The community leaders viewed the Rio Grande as the savior of their cities' growth and prosperity. Without it, the basin's economy would flounder, the population would slump into a severe decline, and economies would grind to a halt. Many entrepreneurs, along with the city planners who had pinned their hopes and personal fortunes on continued growth, also demanded more water and electricity.

In 1962 government and civic leaders recognized that increasing demands for water exceeded the river's flow, and they felt it was necessary to add water to the river. Congress authorized the construction of the enormous San Juan–Chama canal, which carries an additional flow of water diverted from the Colorado River to the Rio Grande north of Albuquerque. Yet even this was not sufficient. It was clear to everyone that the Rio Grande would need to work even harder.

More Dams

More water could be guaranteed only by constructing dams capable of storing and redirecting the water supply. During the 1950s and 1960s, dam construction along the Rio Grande accelerated dramatically to meet urban demands for water. As an example of two Rio Grande cities' needs for water, the city of Albuquerque has annual rights to 48,200 AF of water, the equivalent of 17.4 billion gallons, and the city of El Paso annually draws 52,000 AF, or 18.7 billion gallons.

Although Elephant Butte Dam and Caballo Dam were already harnessing and diverting much of the Rio Grande's

San Juan–Chama Diversion Project

According to a U.S. Bureau of Reclamation study, the total amount of water that is annually depleted from the Rio Grande from the point at which the river enters New Mexico to the Elephant Butte Dam totals about 560,000 acre-feet. This total includes evaporation from the river and dam as well as draws for irrigation. So much is lost that the city of Albuquerque and other smaller cities north of the dam found themselves in need of more water than the river could deliver.

In 1962, to resolve this long-standing problem, Congress authorized the construction of an enormous canal named the San Juan–Chama Project (SJCP). This canal was designed to bring Colorado River water from the San Juan Mountains in southwestern Colorado seventy-eight miles across the Continental Divide and into the Rio Grande seventy-six miles north of Albuquerque. Through this stretch, a series of three tunnels, totaling twenty-six miles, were carved under the Continental Divide to the Rio Grande basin. The water flows through this series of tunnels at about 650 cubic yards per second.

The primary purpose of the 96,200 AF that is annually delivered down the SJCP is to provide needed water for irrigation as well as for municipal, domestic, and industrial uses in the middle Rio Grande basin north of Elephant Butte Reservoir. Project water also provides incidental recreation and fish and wildlife benefits. Regulations require that all of this additional water be consumed north of Elephant Butte Reservoir.

water for urban and agricultural use, the need for more water became readily apparent. Three additional major dams were constructed to accommodate the river basin's urban expansion: one at Falcon, Texas, in 1953; another at Cochiti, New Mexico, in 1960; and a third at Del Rio, Texas, in 1969. These five major dams were immediately followed by an additional twenty smaller dams needed to meet the water needs of agriculture and new cities.

As modern cities grew, the river was also asked to deliver electricity to power factory machinery, homes, modern office buildings, schools, hospitals, shopping malls, and millions of air conditioners. Modern urbanites also wanted to illuminate the desert night with lights so they could attend after-dinner activities such as theatrical performances, sporting events, and concerts.

To meet the need for electricity, the Elephant Butte and Caballo Dams were retrofitted with electricity-generating turbines to provide hydroelectric energy, and all new dams were designed with turbines. The principle of generating hydroelectricity at dams is relatively simple and has the benefit of operating pollution-free because no fossil fuels, such as coal or oil, are burned in the process.

Dams are fitted with turbines that spin to produce electricity. In the interior of a concrete dam, water from the dam's reservoir falls through enormous intake pipes and strikes large metal fins, similar to propellers, causing the turbines to spin. As the turbines spin, they generate electrons that are transported along high-tension lines to nearby cities that consume them.

The Elephant Butte Dam is the largest structure on the Rio Grande. It separates the river from the largest lake in New Mexico, the Elephant Butte Lake.

River Industries

Industries along the Rio Grande began profiting from the river in ways other than receiving electricity. Many industries that manufacture goods in factories or extract precious metals from mines draw water directly from the river and use it in a variety of ways to produce products. For this reason, most mines and factories are located on the banks of the river for easy access to the water and for the return of used water.

Gold and silver mines are concentrated along the upper reaches of the Rio Grande near the river's source in Colorado. Enormous quantities of water are used in an extraction process for gold and silver called flotation milling. Carl Mount, senior environmental protection specialist of the Division of Minerals and Geology for the state of Colorado, describes flotation milling this way:

> Mine operators dump tons of crushed earth and rock into large holding tanks filled with water, specific oils, a mixture of chemicals, and detergents. This mixture, called slurry, is then injected with air in the form of bubbles that cause the flakes of precious metals to adhere to the oil and chemicals and to float to the surface. The precious metals, such as gold and silver, are then skimmed off the top leaving the slurry behind that is deposited into large holding ponds. [17]

Another industry that draws an enormous volume of water from the Rio Grande is the textile industry. Cotton grown along the lower two segments of the river is picked and trucked to textile factories close to the river. Factories draw millions of gallons of water from the Rio Grande for an initial cleaning of the cotton, which is done in enormous vats that clean and then spin the cotton to extract most of the water. Once cleaned, the cotton is spun and woven into a variety of different large bolts. These are then immersed in vats of water and bleach to remove any natural color prior to being sent to the dyeing vats. The dyeing vats are filled with water and measured amounts of dyes that permanently set the color of the cotton fabric. A final rinse follows the dyeing process before the fabric is dried and converted into a variety of clothing and linen items.

Chemical and food processing plants along the lower Rio Grande also draw heavily from the river. Much of the water used in both of these industries is used for the cleaning and sanitizing of equipment and for a variety of filtration procedures. Both industries are required to maintain high standards for sanitation and the elimination of impurities that might otherwise contaminate their products. Water drawn from the river is often used to dilute solvents flushed through pipelines and mixing vats after one batch of food or chemicals is manufactured to ensure that the next batch will not be contaminated. Water is also used in filtration processes for both industries to separate one particular component from all others.

The Rio Grande is a workhorse of a river that occasionally is called on to entertain as well. Within the past few decades, the river has become a favorite source of recreation for boaters, white-water rafters, fishermen, and swimmers.

Recreation on the Rio Grande

As the larger dams were built and their reservoirs filled with billions of gallons of water, the Rio Grande provided yet another value for those living along its banks as a place of recreation. The reservoirs created by many of the larger dams changed the recreational offerings of the Rio Grande by creating large, calm lakes that could be enjoyed by millions of visitors who annually come for boating, waterskiing, jet skiing, scuba diving, swimming, fishing, hiking, and camping. The most notable recreation reservoir and the most popular on the river is Elephant Butte Reservoir in New Mexico.

Elephant Butte Lake, which is the largest lake on the Rio Grande, is 45 miles long, 4 miles wide, and has a fluctuating surface area of about 180 square miles. In addition to its wide offerings of water sports, its sandy beaches, quiet

coves, and lakeside trails provide locations for quiet rest and destinations for wildlife and birdwatchers. Vacationers also find full-service marinas, camping areas, designated recreational vehicle hookup areas, and enough open water for cabin cruisers and houseboats.

White-water rafting is one of many recreational activities that visitors find on the Rio Grande.

The lake is most of all a favorite fishing haven. It is known for its trophy-size bass along with northern pike, catfish, sunfish, bluegill, crappie, perch, walleye, carp, and occasionally rainbow trout. Boaters, whether trolling for fish or taking in the scenery, enjoy the lake's hourglass shape with big upper and lower sections connected by a four-mile stretch of the Rio Grande named the Narrows.

The lake is also a business. Hundreds of people earn their living at the lake providing all of the recreational services needed for Fourth of July weekends that can attract as many as one hundred thousand travelers. Motels, restaurants, boat rental businesses, fishing tackle shops, grocery stores, gas stations, and dozens of smaller services generate annual revenues exceeding $200 million. The parks department, which manages the dam's recreational concessions, is proud of the glistening lake, its two hundred miles of shoreline, a bountiful array of sport fish, and camping concessions that put the Rio Grande to work for the estimated 1 million vacationers who annually enjoy this beautiful playground.

Environmentalists, biologists, and dozens of communities living downriver from the dam, however, do not always share this same enthusiasm for the economics of the lake or the lake's popularity as a recreational site. Many groups are concerned with the health and overuse of the Rio Grande's water. As the twenty-first century begins, there is increasing evidence that this nineteen-hundred-mile-long workhorse flowing through one of America's largest desert regions is suffering as a result of too many demands being made on its finite water supply.

4

$\bullet\bullet\bullet\bullet\bullet\bullet\bullet\bullet\bullet\bullet$

The Overtapped Oasis

As the twenty-first century pushes forward, the Rio Grande is acquiring the tired and worn-out look of an over-tapped oasis. Stretched to the limit by water demands for crop irrigation, cities, and factories, long tracts of this great river are annually reduced to dry washes during the summer. Those dependent on the river's steady flow are desperate to find alternatives while many local species of wildlife, which once flourished, are now disappearing at an alarming rate.

Records kept by hydrologists measuring the river's annual flow tell an instructive and poignant story. Prior to 1945 the waters of the Rio Grande continuously flowed into the Gulf of Mexico. During the summer of 1945, however, for the first time ever recorded, the great river ran out of water several miles short of its usual plunge into the sea. Since that foreboding summer, the river has increasingly failed to reach the sea; since 1990, it has failed ten times.

The system of dams and irrigation canals constructed along the Rio Grande, which were symbols of a progressive Southwest during much of the twentieth century, are now viewed by many as symbols of misguided planning and poor

Each year the Rio Grande loses water due to demands for its resources. Wildlife species are also vanishing in habitats surrounding the river.

judgment. Each year, an average of 790,000 acre-feet of water is released from the Elephant Butte and Caballo Dams for delivery to farmers and towns in southern New Mexico, Mexico, and Texas. Most years, by the time the Rio Grande reaches the city of Presidio, Texas, just north of its confluence with the Conchos River, it is entirely depleted.

Rangers working at Big Bend National Park in Texas observe, "By the time the Rio Grande leaves El Paso, so much water has been diverted that the riverbed between El Paso and Presidio often lies dry." [18] It is primarily the water of the Conchos River and additional downriver tributaries that carry the Rio Grande farther downriver but not as far as the Gulf of Mexico.

According to a press release by American Rivers, a national nonprofit conservation organization dedicated to protecting and restoring American rivers,

> The Rio Grande faces potential ecological collapse due to excessive consumption of its limited water supply and over-engineering of its fragile riverbed and riverside habitat. Throughout the 20th century, river management for the Rio Grande has meant channelization, levee construction, destruction of native vegetation, dredging, and water diversion. [19]

In 1993 Congressman George Miller aptly summed up the attitude that has brought the Rio Grande to the brink of collapse when he observed that federal, state, and local attitudes toward the river had been "driven by the notion that if any water reached the ocean, it was wasted. So you ought to grab it and put it somewhere else." [20]

Dams Versus Wildlife

The large concrete dams along the Rio Grande are responsible for more adverse consequences to its ecosystem than any other single factor. Their presence alters the river's natural flow, causing distinct, well-documented problems. Scientific journals widely report the dams' impact on downriver ecosystems generally, and the fish populations specifically.

Water masters, the engineers who determine when to store and when to release water from the river's many hydroelectric dams, usually regulate water flow based on consumer need for hydroelectricity. Disrupting the natural and continuous flow of the Rio Grande prior to the construction of the dams, water masters now release water in intermittent, massive bursts timed to coincide with peak power consumption. Sudden bursts of water are damaging to the river's ecosystems. Such blasts of cascading water crashing on the riverbed create enough friction to physically scour delicate aquatic organisms and displace or kill fish populations.

Withholding water from the streambed for long or frequent periods is equally ruinous. River segments downriver from large dams can quickly dry up. Death can come quickly to riparian vegetation and stranded fauna, especially amphibians and fish, crucial to the river's ecosystem. In addition to the aquatic wildlife, migrating birds that normally stop to feed and rest along the river's estuaries must go elsewhere when they arrive and discover a dry river.

The unnatural release of water is only one of the dams' many failings. Their monolithic presence, which functions like a gargantuan concrete plug in the river, is another. Fish populations, a necessary link in the river's food chain as well as a source of food and recreation for humans, are incapable of swimming past the dams in either direction. As fish populations diminish, other plants and animals dependent on the fish also suffer.

Dam designers ordinarily attempt to build fish ladders, a series of concrete steps bathed in cascading water on the sides of dams, to provide passage in both directions for migrating fish. Such ladders, however, are not feasible on large dams the size of Elephant Butte. Without fish ladders, the migrating fish are permanently cut off from upriver spawning grounds. Phil Hastings, curator of marine vertebrates at the Scripps Institution of Oceanography in La Jolla, California, observes that

> dams lacking fish ladders force fish to survive in side canyons. Although some spawning does take place there, the survival rate is low because the fry are forced out into the main river before they are strong enough to survive. That is why parents attempt to swim upriver to locate smaller, calmer, and better sheltered streams that protect their young while they grow.[21]

The prospects for swimming downstream are no better. Many fish living in the large reservoirs are sucked through the dam in one of two ways: through an intake pipe feeding water to the hydroelectric generators or through one of the dam's floodgates, which release water through enormous pipes that channel the water through the dam and into the river below. In either case, the chances for fish surviving are poor. According to Hastings, fish sucked into the turbines "disintegrate from the spinning turbine blades." He adds that that the survival rate of those forced through the floodgates is "not much better because of the turbulence in the pipes, sudden changes of temperature and pressure, and the impact hitting the river at high speeds when exhausted from the pipes." [22]

Fish ladders on the sides of dams supply routes for migrating fish. Without these structures, migrating fish are cut off from spawning grounds and chances for survival are poor.

The Plight of the Silvery Minnow

The tiny silvery minnow, just four inches long, has become the poster fish for the beleaguered Rio Grande. The silvery minnow, once one of the most abundant fish species in the Rio Grande, is the last kind of minnow remaining in the river. Increased pollution and reduced flow is killing off the minnows and is endangering the health of other species within the entire riparian system. The U.S. Fish and Wildlife Service (USFWS) held a meeting in 1992 to warn water users of the rapid demise of this fish, listed as an endangered species in 1994, and others.

Once teaming by the millions, the endangered minnow now lives only in a small fraction of its original habitat along the Rio Grande. The disappearance of this fish is a red flag to biologists that the big river is in jeopardy of losing its ecological balance.

The recent decline of the silvery minnow is triggering a swift and immediate response. Biologists conducted surveys in July and August 2002 that showed over 90 percent of the remaining population is concentrated in a small stretch of river just above Elephant Butte Reservoir, which is the most likely stretch to go dry. The USFWS considers the situation to be an emergency.

Hydrologists and biologists know that the decline of the silvery minnow is merely a symptom that the river itself is dying. Immediate action to protect not only the minnow but also the multitude of life the river supports is needed. But the Bureau of Reclamation and the Army Corps of Engineers, two federal agencies that oversee the well-being of the river, assert that they have almost no discretion to change the way the river is operated. They can only make recommendations to politicians as to how to prevent the death of the river and the species dependent on it.

Wildlife is not the only victim of dams; the very water in the dams is also adversely affected. River water, in its natural state, is intended by nature to be constantly on the move from source to outfall. Impounding it behind dams has unfortunate consequences.

Dams Versus Water

The major criticism that hydrologists level against large dams is the high evaporation rate of water in their reservoirs. Water naturally flowing down the Rio Grande typically remains within the confines of a narrow riverbed with relatively little surface area exposed to the hot desert sun, which voraciously evaporates water. The huge, expansive lakes that trail behind dams, however, expose vast areas of surface water to the sun, causing far more evaporation of this precious resource than occurs in the natural river. Journalist Tania Soussan, investigating the water shortages along the Rio Grande, reported in July 2000 that "evaporation at Elephant Butte reservoir, for example, has averaged 180,000 acre-feet [6.48 trillion gallons] annually over the past 15 years. This volume of evaporation exceeds the water extracted from the river by the four largest American cities along the river."[23]

Dams play a part in the degradation of the Rio Grande. Water from the Elephant Butte reservoir has steadily evaporated because large areas of surface water are exposed to the sun.

The higher rates of evaporation that occur at all dams contribute to higher salinity levels as well. All freshwater rivers contain some salt. As water evaporates, salt is left behind, increasing the water's salinity. Plant and animal life then become ill and even die from the increased levels of salinity. According to the *Texas Center for Policy Studies/Dams on the Rio Grande,* published in 1998, "Increasing salinity in the main stem, and especially the two major international reservoirs (Falcon and Amistad) has serious implications throughout the basin for long-term agricultural and municipal water use." [24] The rise in salinity is so severe that another study discovered that saltwater-tolerant fish species, which typically remain in the ocean, have proliferated as far as 170 miles upriver from the Gulf of Mexico.

Dams are not the sole cause of the degradation of the Rio Grande and its habitats. The many cities and factories that withdraw water from the river very often expel the used water back into the river along with pollutants that range from human excrement to highly toxic chemicals that are byproducts of many manufacturing processes.

Urban Pollution

Scientists studying the quality of the Rio Grande's water point to several troubling sources of pollution. The one most immediately troublesome to the medical profession is high concentrations of fecal matter.

In 1994 Lisa LaRocque, director of a project to test the quality of the river's water over a fifteen-hundred-mile stretch, commented to reporter Bruce Selcraig, "To be honest, I don't see anything comforting about the results. . . . The river's worst health problem continues to be high levels of fecal coliform." [25] Fecal coliform is a bacterium found in stomach linings that is excreted by mammals and birds. Its presence in the water of the Rio Grande comes from wild animals, cattle, and, primarily, from untreated raw human sewage. Fecal coliform also indicates the presence of organisms that carry potentially deadly diseases such as hepatitis, dysentery, typhoid, and cholera.

The highest concentrations come from specific sources, such as city sewage pipes. Raw sewage in the river has been a problem for many years because the largest cities on the Mexican side have antiquated sewage treatment plants or none at all. In Nuevo Laredo, for example, where officials say the city's first sewage treatment plant is at least a year from completion, about 70 percent of its half-million people flush their wastes directly into the Rio Grande. "Some parts of the river are so dirty," says U.S. health coordinator Craig Heacock, "that it's even dangerous to have anyone test it." [26]

Dr. Laurance Nickey, director of the El Paso City-County Health and Environmental District, makes a similar observation about the Mexican city of Juárez, just across the river from El Paso. According to Nickey, Juárez officials have told him that 55 million gallons of raw sewage and industrial pollutants leave the city of 2 million each day. "They discharge it into irrigation canals that parallel the

Researchers test the polluted water of the Rio Grande. Raw sewage is found in parts of the river and it can carry potentially fatal diseases.

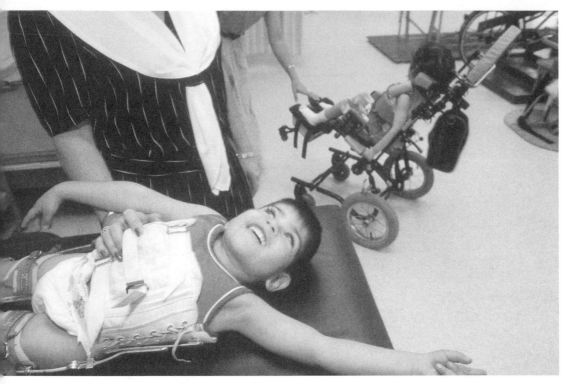

A child suffering from a spinal disorder thought to have been caused by polluted water waits in a clinic in Brownsville, Texas.

Rio Grande for 18 miles and serve some 60,000 acres of farmland. When it's not used for irrigation, the canals are rediverted into the Rio Grande—in fact, a few miles upstream of Fort Hancock [Texas]." [27]

Although the presence of fecal coliform from urban discharge of raw sewage is a very serious problem, recent studies indicate that toxic chemical pollution may pose an even worse long-term health risk.

Industrial Effluents

Industrial effluents, water contaminated by mine and factory production containing high levels of toxic chemicals, are increasing along the Rio Grande. Of particular concern to health officials are heavy metals, such as cadmium, mercury, iron, and lead, that are capable of remaining in the environment at high levels for a long time. When ingested by living organisms, they are known to cause cancer and birth defects in humans and animals.

In January 2000 journalist Russell Gold, wrote an article, for the *San Antonio Express-News,* about Dr. Jim Earhart of the Rio Grande International Study Center. In the piece, Earhart reports that a 1997 Texas Natural Resources Conservation Commission (TNRCC) study leads to the conclusion that pollutants from clothing manufacturers are making their way into the river. Earhart states, "These toxic chemicals . . . are coming primarily from garment manufacturers. Unregulated discharges along the banks of creeks that feed into the Rio Grande are the principal threat to water quality."[28]

Another journalist, Cadence Mertz, reported in October 1999 that, according to the TNRCC, there are over twelve hundred warehouses in the Laredo area, many of which have been built near tributaries without protection for spills or other safeguards. In her article Mertz mentions that Laredo city officials discovered

> a mountain of sludge, concrete, plastic bags, old tires, used sofas and empty industrial containers next to a channel running into the river. Included in the rubble were 75 empty containers of muriatic acid, a chemical used to clean air conditioners and toilets that can be harmful if inhaled.[29]

Effluent from mines along the upper Rio Grande can be just as toxic as that from downriver industries. Modern mines, which use flotation milling to extract precious metals, create large holding ponds that contain a variety of toxic substances. According to Carl Mount, "The liquid residue in these ponds, called tailings, slowly seep into the water table and eventually find their way to small creeks and streams that feed into the Rio Grande."[30] Mines that use older extraction technologies employ a variety of heavy metals to extract gold, silver, and copper. Much of these heavy metals remain in cast-off rubble. Water that flows through some of the mines near Creede, Colorado, for example, mixes with the cast-off rubble. As a result, many small creeks that feed into the Rio Grande contain levels of zinc, dissolved cadmium, arsenic, and lead well above state water quality standards. For example, in West Willow Creek lead contamination is eighty-two times the allowable levels. In May 1998 the U.S. Geologic Survey (USGS) concluded,

> Highly elevated concentrations of antimony, arsenic, cadmium, copper, lead, mercury, silver, and zinc were detected in bed sediment from Willow Creek and the Rio Grande, downstream from the Creede, Colorado, Mining District. [31]

Endangered Species

High concentrations of toxic effluent, coupled with problems caused by dams, threaten the river's wildlife. The first species to show signs of ill health in any river is the fish. One type of fish, the silvery minnow, is considered an indicator species, a species that is most vulnerable to changes in the environment. The silvery minnow of the Rio Grande is in danger of extinction. In April 2000 Rebecca Wodder, president of American Rivers, commented, "New water diversions, flood control projects, and dam operations that drastically change the river's natural flow could serve the death sentence to the silvery minnow and other native fish and wildlife of the Rio Grande." [32] In April 2002 a group of ichthyologists, scientists who study fish, concurred with Wodder, adding, "In all, thirteen of the river's twenty-four native fish species are threatened with the possibility of extinction." [33]

Over the past two decades, researchers have understood the link between declining fish populations and declining quality of the river's water. Much of the water is polluted by toxins that enter upstream, affecting fish as the chemicals flow far downriver. An analysis for the Environmental Protection Agency (EPA) by Dr. Earhart found that toxic chemicals flow far from their source, as he recently noted: "Of the thirty toxic chemicals found to exceed various governmental screening levels between El Paso and Brownsville, nineteen were as far south as the Laredo area." [34] The toxins had traveled about two hundred miles. Earhart also analyzed tissue samples of fish found dead in the water to determine if they died from toxic overdose and, if so, what toxic chemicals they were ingesting. His results revealed that "twelve toxic chemicals were found to exceed screening [high but acceptable] levels in fish tissue."[35] Of perhaps

Algae Blooms

Changes to the characteristics of the Rio Grande can be stressful to the entire river. Wendell Barber, a biologist and water-quality specialist working for several water commissions in the Rio Grande basin, was the first to notice an imbalance in naturally occurring algae called golden algae, that has caused short-term fish kills at several spots along the river.

Golden algae naturally occurs in the Rio Grande but generally not in high enough concentrations to be toxic to fish species. According to Barber, however, writing for the Colorado River Municipal Water District's website, "Normally, the bluegreen and green algae, which have chlorophyll, compete with Golden Algae for nutrients in the water. Recently, however, the bluegreen and green algae have been dying out allowing the Golden Algae to multiply to toxic levels." Barber says experts believe "it may be related to sudden temperature swings, such as the one we had just before this kill started."

Barber goes on to say that, "without competition, the Goldens bloom and multiply disproportionately, as their competitors die and become nutrients. The blooming Golden Algae are doubly dangerous for fish. First, they produce a natural detergent and release it into the water, usually visible as a tall stiff foam and evident from the 'slick' feel of the water. Fish secrete slime to protect their gills, and the detergents wash it off. The fish's body then works overtime to produce more slime, but the damaged gills begin to hemorrhage and the fish begins to suffocate, unable to get oxygen from the water. . . . If a fish is able to get out of the algae at this point, its gills may be scarred, but it can survive. However, in a very short time, the toxin's second attack begins as it works its way into the circulatory and nervous systems of the fish. . . . Fish kills of this type have been seen all over Texas."

Golden algae blooms are a forewarning to biologists. When these are detected, biologists recommend a quick flooding of the river to reduce toxic effects on fish.

even greater concern, Earhart revealed EPA results of fish analysis that detected "arsenic levels in a fillet of bass were 11.1 times the Environmental Protection Agency's tissue criterion near the Jefferson Street Water Treatment Plant— the sole source of Laredo's drinking water." [36]

Dry rivers also equate to disappearing fish. As long as segments of the Rio Grande dry up, fish will cease spawning and their populations will decline. It is the opinion of the EPA that the "decline of fish species in the Middle Rio Grande probably began in 1916 when the gates at Elephant Butte Dam were [built]." [37] Construction of the dam signaled the beginning of an era of mainstream Rio Grande dam construction that resulted in five major dams, each of which narrowed fish habitats.

Water Disputes with Mexico

The problems of dams, pollution, and water shortages have combined over the years to cause occasional friction between the United States and Mexico. Sharing a twelve-hundred-mile stretch of the Rio Grande as well as sharing water from tributaries deep inside of each country has led to resentment on both sides that has necessitated international water treaties. In spite of treaties, however, friction continues as both countries try to find equitable solutions to the water problems, most of all, water shortages.

The major point of conflict between the United States and Mexico revolves around each country's right to the Rio Grande's water. This is a tricky issue since each country has the headwaters of several major tributaries that flow to the Rio Grande. Mexico initially objected to the construction of the Elephant Butte Dam because of justifiable fears that very little of the Rio Grande south of the dam might ever reach Mexico. To allay such concerns, the first water treaty was ratified by the two countries in 1907, guaranteeing Mexico an annual allotment of 60,000 AF from the Rio Grande. Mexico, which has the headwaters of the Conchos River and five other smaller tributaries deep within its borders, guaranteed in 1944 to allow one-third of its rivers' water to flow to their confluences with the Rio Grande, an estimated annual allotment of 350,000 AF.

These two treaties seemed to work well until about the 1970s, when the first serious shortages, caused by excessive use of the river's water and a few serious droughts, occurred. Suddenly, each country accused the other of violating the treaties. At the heart of the debate was a growing water debt of 1.5 million AF that Mexico owed the United States.

Neither side seems to be in an agreeable mood over the dispute. Reporter Jan Reid interviewed Rogelio Bejarno, the head of one Mexican irrigation district, who explained that if farmers do not use their allocations of water, they lose their rights to it in the future. Bejarno candidly told the reporter, "It does not bother me a bit if Texans are upset. Our people have suffered. They've had to reduce planting. Here, if the land is not productive and people don't use their irrigation rights, they lose the water. It's reassigned. Many have given up." [38]

Some on the U.S. side feel just as upset with Mexico. Susan Combs, the agriculture commissioner for Texas, declared in an interview with Reid, "They've got a governor in Chihuahua [Mexico] who says, 'If the rain falls here, it's mine.' He does not believe he has to be a partner in the treaty." [39]

5

. . . .

Working Toward
Water Security

Never has the competition for the Rio Grande's water been so intense. All competing parties share keen but often conflicting views on who ought to have the water, how much each deserves, and how it can best serve the interests of everyone within the river's vast multinational basin. Satisfying each group is the challenge of the twenty-first century, and implicit in this challenge is the clear reality that the river cannot provide enough water to satisfy the needs and wants of each group. Regardless of the enormity of the task, all groups understand the importance of taking steps toward achieving water security.

One point of agreement, which is acknowledged by all parties, is the necessity of striking compromises. Growing cities and farms cannot expect to increase their water allocations as they have in the past. Environmentalists, the newcomers to the struggles over the finite water supply, advocate an increase of water flow to protect fish and other wildlife, even at the expense of urban and economic growth. Unprecedented urban growth in the midst of a scorching desert, they assert, makes unreasonable and excessive demands on water and electricity. Watering of the scorching-hot desert to produce water-gluttonous crops such as lettuce, oranges, pecans, onions, and peppers is equally unreasonable and excessive.

To evenly spread the wealth of the river's resources throughout the Rio Grande basin, current management of the river must include modifying and compromising everyone's expectations of what the river can reasonably provide.

Rapids crash against rocks in the Rio Grande. Farmers, city planners, and environmentalists disagree as to how the water of the river should be allocated.

Sandra Postel, author of the book *Last Oasis*, makes the case for changing how people and governments in America's Southwest think about and utilize their water:

> In the past, decisions about water have been guided by a simple formula which said "estimate human demands for water, and build a new project to meet it." That equation was simple, and it worked as long as water was abundant. But it's not working anymore because water is becoming scarce and delivery systems too costly. Moving to "a culture of conservation" requires a major change in the way people think about water. [40]

Sprinkler systems are now used to meet the demand for irrigation. Drip irrigation and plastic sheeting are other methods used along the Rio Grande.

Improving Irrigation Techniques

Farmers are beginning to step forward to increase irrigation efficiency. During the early decades of the twentieth century, water from the Rio Grande was so plentiful that the two most common irrigation techniques used by farmers were flooding and open-ditch irrigation. Flooding, as

the name suggests, involves immersing fields in a bath of water, which creates temporary lakes in the midst of desert farmlands. Open-ditch irrigation, on the other hand, floods ditches on both sides of rows of plants, allowing the water to saturate the roots. Although more economical than flooding, the water loss is still quite high. In either case, hydrologists estimate that between one-third and one-half of the water never reaches the roots. Evaporation robs most of it, and some of it saturates soil beyond the reach of roots.

Today, as the demand for water skyrockets and the availability declines, such inefficient forms of irrigation can no longer be tolerated. Shortages of water for agriculture have forced farmers to rethink how they irrigate their crops. Amy Souers, writing for the environmental organization American Rivers, makes the point that "diversions for municipal and agricultural use already claim nearly 95 percent of the Rio Grande's average annual flow. Irrigators are using outdated and inefficient practices that waste significant amounts of water." [41] Statistics compiled by Forest Guardians, a nonprofit organization dedicated to protecting the forests and rivers of the Southwest, confirm Souers's report. According to Forest Guardians, two stretches of farmland in New Mexico rank as the worst and the fifth-worst in the nation for the percent of water actually delivered by irrigation to the roots of crops—a meager 9 percent for the worst and 29 percent for the other. Statistics supplied by Forest Guardians also claim that in 1998, the Middle Rio Grande Conservancy District diverted 679,000 acre-feet of water to supply less than 52,000 acres of farmland, which equals about 470,076 gallons per acre.

The first new irrigation technology tried along the Rio Grande was drip irrigation. This technology, now widely used in citrus, sugarcane, and pecan orchards, delivers water directly to the root area of each tree or plant by means of narrow plastic tubes running on or below the soil's surface. This method ensures a minimum loss of water to evaporation or percolation beyond the reach of roots. A researcher for the Texas Water Resources Institute, Bob

Wiedenfeld, comments on his findings using drip irrigation for sugarcane: "Flood irrigation isn't practical because it requires so much water. . . . Sugarcane yields were 45 tons per acre with drip irrigation, compared to 40 tons per acre with flood irrigation. The drip irrigation used 30% less water." [42]

Drip irrigation, which is successful for large plants and trees, is not, however, as efficient for low-growing row crops such as carrots, beans, lettuce, squash, and peppers. For these crops, which are grown close together, two new technologies have been developed, one using low-pressure sprinklers and the other using plastic sheeting to create tent environments under which young crops grow.

Low-pressure sprinklers can perform almost as well as drip methods when they are designed properly. Traditional high-pressure irrigation sprinklers spray water high into the air to cover as large a land area as possible. The problem is that as water spends time in the air, it evaporates and blows off course before reaching the plants. In contrast, new low-energy sprinklers deliver water in small doses through nozzles positioned just above the ground. Numerous farmers in Texas who have installed such sprinklers have found that their plants absorb 90 to 95 percent of the water that leaves the sprinkler nozzle.

Thin plastic sheeting placed over cultivated rows immediately following the planting of seeds is another new technology. Tenting newly planted crops conserves water that normally evaporates because it is captured under the plastic covering and drips back on the plants when nighttime temperatures drop. Tenting requires irrigation by either open ditch or one of several sprinklers placed under the tenting.

Urban Water Conservation

Agriculture consumes the lion's share of the Rio Grande's water, but it does not take sole responsibility for all water waste. Water shortages over the past two decades have sparked a great deal of public discussion over urban water

A New Water Ethic

Not everyone is convinced that science and technology alone are capable of solving all of the problems that swirl around the use of Rio Grande water. More efficient high-tech irrigation systems, Xeriscape landscaping, water recycling, and low-flush toilets may only have a modest impact on a large problem. Even removing all of the dams, as some of the more strident conservation groups have suggested, would not necessarily solve all of the problems that have arisen since the 1950s.

Sandra Postel, author of *Last Oasis,* introduces a new approach to solving the problems of rivers such as the Rio Grande, which are depleted of their water before reaching the sea. She believes that the only way to rejuvenate the Rio Grande is by teaching people to adopt a new water ethic, or attitude toward water use. Simply stated, Postel's water ethic involves respecting water as a limited and essential commodity that must be used sparingly. The following are three aspects of her water ethic that she believes will help save the river:

• Charging the true price for water— Agriculture and industries are not charged the true cost of water. Both receive significant discounts and, as a result, are not sufficiently motivated to conserve. Their cost for water must be the true cost.
• Population redistribution—The desert is not an environment suitable for large urban populations. Large population centers should exist in temperate climates.
• Living within our means—Borrowing from the ethic of "waste not, want not," water should be viewed as money and not thoughtlessly thrown away.

use as well. Everyone seems to agree that enormous volumes are being wasted through inefficient use and that steps can be taken in homes and downtown public property to conserve water.

The El Paso Water Utility District estimates that each person in its city uses an average of 163 gallons of water per day. This figure includes water for drinking, bathing, washing dishes, watering lawns, and dozens of other standard household uses. The water district has established a goal to reduce use to 160 gallons per person per day. Although such a savings is relatively small, water district officials view it as a first step that will be followed by further reductions.

Travis Miller, a Texas A&M University agronomist and drought expert, agrees. Noting that Juárez residents average only 88 gallons of water per day, he believes that use in El Paso can comfortably drop well below the 160-gallon mark because "people can live quite nicely on just 75 gallons a day."[43] But to achieve this goal, El Pasoans would have to forgo lush home gardens, swimming pools, long showers, and washing their cars, as well as implement a ten-year phase-out of existing residential and commercial lawns throughout the city.

To achieve reductions in urban water consumption, El Paso implemented a lawn watering restriction in 1990 that limited lawn watering to early mornings and late evenings to reduce evaporation. Since its inception, the El Paso Water Utility District has saved a total of 30.4 billion gallons of water, more than a one-year supply. To enforce the rule, El Paso issued 121 citations in 1995 for wasting water that ranged from fifty to five hundred dollars. Another water-saving step the city took was to change the city building code in 1991 to require builders to use water-conserving, low-flush toilets. Old standard toilets use 5 to 6 gallons of water to flush while modern ones use just 1.6 gallons. Estimated savings have been about 185 million gallons.

To achieve even greater water savings, El Pasoans are being asked to voluntarily replace lawns and lush garden vegetation around new homes and buildings in favor of Xeriscape landscaping. Derived from the Greek word *xeros,* meaning "dry," and combined with *landscape,* Xeriscape is a landscaping strategy that provides a varied and colorful garden using drought-tolerant plants that do not require a large amount of water. Some people, such as Travis Miller, ask even more of citizens when he voices the opinion that

in the rural areas southeast of El Paso, where I live, we don't have lawns. Water is for drinking and to grow food, not to create an unnatural environment at the expense of the region's ancient aquifers and of the river. El Pasoans and everyone must recognize we live in a desert, and our precious water cannot be wasted on lawns, swimming pools, golf courses, jeans washing plants, and other water intensive industries. [44]

Laundering Water

Industry is also motivated to do its part to achieve water security. "We recycle and reuse our dirty shirts . . . we launder them. You have to learn how to launder water," [45] proclaimed professor Hillel Shuval of Hebrew University, in Jerusalem, in July 2000. Recycling used water so it can be used a second or third time, an idea that germinated in water-starved Israel during the 1950s, has finally arrived along the Rio Grande—especially below Elephant Butte Dam. Factory owners, environmentalists, scientists, and finally politicians are recognizing the value of recycling water.

One of the first big companies to recognize the value of recycling water in El Paso was American Garment Finishers Corporation, the city's biggest commercial water consumer. This company, like all other textile companies, consumes an enormous volume of water primarily for washing and dyeing fabrics. Prior to 1996, American Garment Finishers Corporation spent a significant amount of money on its water bill. Beginning in 1996, however, the company installed a water recycling system that consists of an enormous multilevel water filtration system. The same year the filtration system was installed, David Ogden-Tamez, working for New Mexico State University, reported that with its ability to reuse water, "The company plans to no longer use city water this spring when the system is fully implemented." [46]

An even more intriguing reuse of water occurred in the city of Harlingen, Texas, in the lower Rio Grande Valley. In a bid to create more jobs, the city appealed to Fruit of the Loom, one of the nation's largest clothing manufacturers, to build a factory in Harlingen. Fruit of the Loom agreed but demanded 3 million gallons of Rio Grande water per day.

Engineers monitor a sewage treatment plant. Companies like Fruit of the Loom are using treated water to conserve water from the Rio Grande.

In this water-strapped South Texas city, civic water engineers met with Fruit of the Loom engineers and proposed a radical water-laundering concept. City engineers first convinced Fruit of the Loom engineers to draw their initial allotment of 3 million gallons from the city's wastewater treatment plant rather than from the river. Then, they recommended that the company invest money in a closed-loop filtration system capable of filtering the used water and returning the cleansed water back for reuse in the manufacturing process. Using this configuration, Fruit of the Loom will demand only occasional makeup water from the Harlingen wastewater plant. Engineers estimate that this continuous reuse of water saves 2,750 AF, or almost 1 billion gallons, of water per year from being diverted from the Rio Grande. System engineer Dennis Raymond states the case for continuously recycling the factory's water: "Because you can't wear out water, we're going to treat and recycle the wastewater back to the factory once again." [47] Recycling is nothing new to Harlingen; its golf course has been irrigated with treated wastewater since 1962.

Factories are not alone in understanding the urgency of recycling used water. Several cities along the Rio Grande utilize aquatic plants as alternatives to conventional wastewater treatment systems. These plants act as filtering systems, removing various toxins from the water. These natural methods have an advantage over typical sewage treatment plants because they are cheaper and do not use any chemicals. Cities in the Rio Grande Valley have used water hyacinths to treat wastewater for industrial reuse since the 1970s. Ric Jensen, information specialist for the Texas Water Resources Institute, believes that, "in the future, natural systems may be useful in treating drinking water from the Rio Grande." [48]

Encouraging and rewarding the conservation and recycling of water constitute the beginnings of a new era of water efficiency. Yet they alone cannot sustain this emerging, environmentally sound undertaking. In order to provide greater impetus to this new approach to solving the problem of water shortages, laws and policies governing water along the Rio Grande must also change.

Updating Water Policies

Moving forward with more efficient, ecologically sound, and sustainable patterns of water use requires major changes in the way water is valued, allocated, and managed. Through state and federal legislation, many economists and agronomists are now changing policies regulating water pricing and allocation.

Dia del Rio

The significance of the Rio Grande is reflected in the annual celebration in El Paso called Dia del Rio, meaning "Day of the River." This festival is a citizen-led event organized by the Rio Grande/Río Bravo Basin Coalition. Dia del Rio is both a call to action and a celebration of the basin's rich cultural and ecological diversity.

The real purpose of the event is to draw public attention to the critical state of the river, its groundwater, its struggling environmental balance, and its threatened wildlife. The annual festival also demonstrates the commitment by citizens in the basin to improve their quality of life. They come together to remind each other of the region's water scarcity, water pollution, and rapid urban growth. This binational event also stresses the need for cross-border cooperation. Many cultures, economic sectors, and interests interact in the Dia del Rio and discuss shared economic and environmental problems. Each of the participating communities implements at least one volunteer activity during the festival. Activities range from tree planting and trash cleanups to public talks and presentations.

According to the Rio Grande/Río Bravo Basin Coalition website, the goals of the festival are to

- Act directly to improve the rivers, native ecosystems, and groundwater in the basin,
- Educate citizens about the grave state of the basin's environment,
- Promote dialogue and cooperation in the basin,
- Demonstrate that people in the basin can unite around issues of common interest,
- And show that the basin's ecology, economy, and cultures depend on one another for sustainability.

The price of water directly affects how much of the precious commodity is used. Low pricing tends to cause people to waste water while very high prices have the opposite effect. In the city of Albuquerque, for example, business and residential users pay $335 per acre-foot for Rio Grande water. Albuquerque farmers, on the other hand, who consume between 80 and 90 percent of New Mexico's water, pay only $28 per acre-foot. Economists and agronomists, who study water pricing for growing food, believe that the amount of water used for irrigating crops would significantly reduce if the price of water to farmers significantly increased. Such increases, they argue, would create incentives for more farmers to convert their cropland to water-efficient drip and plastic-tenting irrigation systems. Legislators in New Mexico are now introducing legislation that will increase the cost of irrigation water in an attempt to force farmers to do just that. Their legislative actions, they believe, may also have the secondary benefit of forcing farmers to switch from low-profit crops, such as alfalfa, which is used as cattle feed, to higher profit foods grown for human consumption.

Legislators are also attacking the antiquated "use-it-or-lose-it" water policy. This policy reduces a farmer's annual allotment of water if he or she fails to use the entire allotment in any one year. This policy, in effect, creates a negative incentive to conserve water, especially at low prices. To circumvent the use-it-or-lose-it policy, legislatures in New Mexico and Texas are now restructuring the sale of water rights in such a way that instead of farmers being penalized for reduced water use, they are being allowed to sell the unused portion of their allotment to someone else. Farmers are encouraged to purchase water-efficient irrigation technologies. Legislators are confident that this change will promote greater conservation of water.

Policy changes such as these two can save farmers money while placing water where it can be better utilized. Conservationists believe that such policy changes can also help heal the Rio Grande. Many environmentalists recommend simply allowing conserved water to remain in the Rio Grande to nurture its suffering river and riparian habitats.

Returning Water to the River

Environmentalists recognize that they too must work hard to find new and innovative ideas to secure water for the river and its wildlife. Leaders have been investigating new alternatives for securing what they view as the Rio Grande's claim to water. "The first order of business is to get water for the river, the river's own entitlement,"[49] says Kevin Bixby, executive director of the Southwest Environmental Center in Las Cruces.

New ideas are being explored to reinstate the river's fair share of water so it will no longer dry up. One option that has already been implemented on a limited basis is buying or leasing water rights from farmers who are able to reduce their water needs through improved irrigation systems. Then, rather than use the purchased or leased water for more irrigation or factory use, environmentalists recommend leaving it in the river to increase its flow. In Taos, New Mexico, where the old use-it-or-lose-it policy is still enforced, Brian Shields, executive director of the advocacy group Amigos Bravos, expresses the opinion: "I think we need to be looking at how to replace that use-it-or-lose-it law and set up either a water bank or some way we can lease water for environmental uses."[50] The water can be leased to an environmental group or a government agency that will then leave the water in the river.

Another option before the state legislature in New Mexico is to amend water laws to require that some portion—perhaps 10 percent—of any water transfer from one entity to another be dedicated to the river. When a water right is transferred from a farm to a housing development, for example, 10 percent of the transferred volume would be set aside to remain in the river unused.

The most successful attempts to return water to the river have meant reevaluating the structures that are most damaging to the river and its wildlife: dams. Ardent conservationists have made calls for the removal of some of the dams on the river without success. Forcing the water master to release more water, however, has been successful. In July 2000, conservationists working for Forest Guardians sued in federal court to force the city of Albuquerque to release an additional 85,000 AF from several upriver reservoirs. In July 2001, the court ordered the water released over several months for the purpose of protecting the habitat of the endangered silvery minnow.

More lawsuits are in the works. Court papers have been filed to stop construction of a newly proposed dam near Los Alamos, New Mexico. Plaintiffs bringing the suit have stopped, for the moment, construction of a seventy-foot-tall, $6.8-million project because of what the courts ruled to be inaccurate engineering information. For now, the Rio Grande will continue to flow freely near Los Alamos.

Increasing the Rio Grande's volume to ensure an adequate water flow downriver, however, may not be enough to push its flow to the sea. Restoring the river's ecosystem is part of the equation envisioned by environmentalists. Such a restoration project requires the removal, or partial removal, of many of the obstructions that presently prevent the water from reaching the Gulf of Mexico.

Unclogging the Rio Grande

Concerned community groups contend that the Rio Grande must be allowed to act like a river with both flood surges and low flows. Without natural flooding, the river becomes clogged with debris. Returning the river to its natural flow, which includes occasional flooding, requires unclogging the obstacles that have developed as a result of insufficient volume ever since the construction of the river's many dams. Since the 1950s, the major obstructions resulting from dams include invasive trees, silt formations, and dislodged riprap, or natural debris such as branches and rocks. Removing these obstructions, environmentalists contend, would bring a variety of wildlife back to life that once played a vital role in the river's balanced ecosystem.

In the river's altered state, native trees like cottonwoods and willows do not have the floodplain conditions, such as rapidly coursing water with low salinity, required to nurture germination. The weakened state of the cottonwoods and willows allow nonnative salt cedars to proliferate and overrun the river and its floodplain. Biologist Ondrea Linderoth-Hummel, president of the New Mexico Riparian Council, recommends the removal of all nonnative trees, especially salt cedars, which have enormous water requirements and

Many obstacles affect the flow of the Rio Grande. Invasive plants and silt obstruct the river, forcing it to change course.

have clogged narrow river channels. One of the main problems with the salt cedar is its unquenchable thirst. A large salt cedar can absorb two hundred gallons of water a day, making it another problem for the Rio Grande, especially when severe droughts grip the Southwest. Salt cedars soak up one-third more water than native plants and offer little for wildlife. In addition to their thirst, salt cedars block the natural flow of the river because of their thickly matted roots and tangle of thick branches that sprout around their trunks. According to John Taylor, a U.S. Fish and Wildlife biologist, "There is structure in a native habitat. There's a ground layer, shrub layer, and canopy. Salt cedar thickets are one block. You almost have to crawl on your belly to get through them." [51]

Since construction of the major dams, the large occasional floods have entirely ceased. One of the many results of this loss is the gradual accumulation of millions of tons of silt, especially where the Rio Grande slows at bends in the river. As silt accumulates, it builds wide bars that grow to heights above the river, forcing the river to change its course. Such changes of the riverbed adversely affect spawning grounds for fish, bury riparian flora, and further warm the water by slowing the river's natural rush.

Riprap, such as riparian trees and bushes, fall or are dislodged in nature's cycle of death and rebirth. This debris, which is generally washed to the ocean by the occasional large flood, now accumulates, creating yet another form of obstruction for river water. Once several large tree trunks embed at a turn in the river, they capture more and more riprap floating by until forming a tight woody mass similar to dams constructed by beavers.

The last ingredient in the complex web for securing water security along the Rio Grande is improving water rights shared between the United States and Mexico.

Improving International Water Rights

Recent disputes between the United States and Mexico over the two water treaties of 1907 and 1944 are in the process of some resolution, but not complete resolution. At the heart of the dispute is America's obligation to allow 60,000 AF of water below the Elephant Butte Dam to flow to Mexico, and Mexico's obligation is to allow annually 350,000 AF of Mexican tributary water to flow to the main channel of the Rio Grande. Over the past several years, some of which have been drought years, Mexico has fallen behind in its obligation by an estimated 1.5 million AF. Texas, which stands to benefit most from repayment, is demanding the full amount.

Because of the drought years, Mexican farmers are suffering and believe their water obligation is unreasonable, especially considering that they are having difficulty irrigating their own crops. Yet Jo Jo White, general manager of the Mercedes irrigation district in Texas, disputes that Mexico does not have the water: "A week ago they had 350,000 to 400,000 acre-feet in the dams. They've had good rains since so the inflow count is growing. It's not substantial but it is adequate. I think they could easily make a transfer of 100,000 or 200,000 acre-feet to the U.S. side." [52]

In a recent effort to remedy tension along the border, a proposal is winning support to scrap both existing treaties and to allow each country to keep all water originating in its own territory. In June 2002 a group of Rio Grande Valley farmers stated in a letter to U.S. secretary of state Colin Powell: "The water crisis for South Texas is worse instead of better. We believe the best solution would be to abrogate the agreement [1944] and start over." [53] Ruben Navarrette Jr., a writer and political analyst for the *Washington Post,* agrees: "A better solution is for the water treaty to be scrapped altogether, as some farmers suggest. This thing is a diplomatic relic, negotiated in an era when the relationship between the two countries was far from even." [54]

Epilogue
· · · · · · · · · · · · ·

A River Thirsting for Water

The present condition of the Rio Grande is well documented. The river has been named on the "Most Threatened Rivers" list by the conservation group American Rivers four times, the most such designations of any American river. Highly altered by dams, levees, channel modifications, excessive depletions, watershed degradation, and wastewater discharges, the Rio Grande continues to be the object of many new development projects by cities and farmers whose water supplies are rapidly dwindling.

Water is a finite commodity and the Rio Grande's supply is no exception. The total volume of water captured within the Rio Grande's basin today has changed little over the past many thousands of years and is unlikely to change appreciably over the next many thousands. The same cannot be said about the population of the region using it. As more and more people pour into the Southwest on both sides of the international border, the amount of water available to each person diminishes. The water of the Rio Grande is inseparably tied to the quality of life in this region and can only support a finite number of people.

Garbage litters the banks of a section of the Rio Grande. Pollution has devastated crops, drinking water, and wildlife.

No problem has more severely impacted the big river than its continuing loss of water to growing cities and to farmers. Mounting demands devastate downriver crops, drinking water, and the river's wildlife. The problems visited upon the Rio Grande over the last half of the twentieth century have created a river that is thirsting for water. Rebecca Wodder, president of the conservation organization American Rivers, states the case for why this trend must stop if a healthy, flowing river is to return:

> The highest and best use of our incredible natural heritage of rivers would be to enhance the quality of life in our communities. Healthy rivers can provide us with open space; close-to-home recreation; safe drinking water; enhanced flood control; and plenty of healthy habitat for fish and wildlife. Today, at the dawn of the 21st century, our rivers deserve a new lease on life.[55]

The push for conservation along the Rio Grande is the call of the twenty-first century. The current economic and social crises resulting from lack of water throughout the border region will obviously not be resolved easily or without significant changes in the way both countries manage the distribution and use of the Rio Grande. The challenge, says Sandra Postel in her book *Last Oasis*, "Is to put as

A rafter steers through a narrow gorge along the Rio Grande. Conservation measures are needed to ensure that the river returns to a healthy state.

much human ingenuity into learning to live in balance with water as we have put into controlling and manipulating it. In the end, the time available to make this shift may prove as precious as water itself." [56]

Ultimately, community leaders must redirect their attitudes toward managing growth in drought-prone areas and recognize water as a renewable but limited and highly valuable commodity.

Notes

· · · · · · · ·

Introduction: The River That Can No Longer Find Its Way to the Sea

1. Quoted in Water in the West, "Rio Grande River Basin," 2002. www.waterinthewest.org.
2. Quoted in Tania Soussan, "Uses Battle for Middle Ground," *Albuquerque Journal,* July 18, 2000.
3. Quoted in Soussan, "Uses Battle for Middle Ground."
4. Quoted in James Pinkerton, "Blockage of Rio Grande's Flow to Gulf Could Have Harmful Effects, Some Fear," *Houston Chronicle,* May 12, 2001.
5. Rio Grande/Río Bravo Basin Coalition, "A Tour of the Rio Grande," February 2002. www.rioweb.org.
6. Forest Guardians, "Water and the Rio Grande," 2002. www.fguardians.org.

Chapter 1: A Desiccated River

7. Brian Tapley, "Rio Grande Delta Marshes," Center for Space Research, April 1999. www.csr.utexas.edu.

Chapter 2: The Ancient Ones

8. Reed McManus, "Way to Go: Rocks of Ages," *Sierra Club Magazine,* July/August 1966, p. 78.
9. Quoted in New Mexico State Engineer Office, "Acequias," July 1997. www.seo.state.nm.us.
10. Quoted in New Mexico State Engineer Office, "Acequias."
11. David Roberts, *In Search of the Old Ones: Exploring the Anasazi World of the Southwest.* New York: Simon & Schuster, 1997, p. 38.
12. Scott A. Elias, *The Ice-Age History of Southwestern National Parks.* Washington, DC: Smithsonian Institution, 1977, p. 28.
13. Elias, *The Ice-Age History of Southwestern National Parks,* p. 30.

14. Edwin Tappan Adney and Howard I. Chapelle, *The Bark Canoes and Skin Boats of North America.* Washington, DC: Museum of History and Technology, Smithsonian Institution, 1964, p. 38.
15. Linda Cordell, "Pueblo Indian Influence," City of Albuquerque, 1996. www.cabq.gov.

Chapter 3: The Workhorse of the Southwest

16. Sherman R. Ellis et al., "Rio Grande Valley, Colorado, New Mexico, and Texas," *American Water Resources Association Bulletin,* vol. 29, no. 4, 1993, p. 619.
17. Carl Mount, Division of Minerals and Geology, Colorado. Telephone interview by author, January 28, 2003.

Chapter 4: The Overtapped Oasis

18. Quoted in Big Bend National Park, "The Rio Grande: The Desert's Lifeblood," January 2003. www.nps. gov.
19. Quoted in, Amy Souers, "Rio Grande Listed Among Nations' Most Endangered Rivers," American Rivers, April 10, 2000. www.amrivers.org.
20. Quoted in Marc Reisner, *Cadillac Desert: The American West and Its Disappearing Water.* New York: Penguin Books, 1993, p. 236.
21. Phil Hastings, Scripps Institution of Oceanography, La Jolla, California. Face-to-face interview by author. July 2, 2002.
22. Hastings interview.
23. Tania Soussan, "Sending Water on to Texas Is Challenge," *Albuquerque Journal,* July 16, 2000.
24. Karen Chapman, "Texas Center for Policy Studies/Dams on the Rio Grande" Texas Water Resources Institute, December 1998. http://twri.tamu.edu.
25. Quoted in Bruce Selcraig, "The Great River Becomes a Great Sewer," *High Country News,* June 13, 1994.
26. Quoted in Selcraig, "The Great River Becomes a Great Sewer."
27. Quoted in Selcraig, "The Great River Becomes a Great Sewer."
28. Russell Gold "Laredo Water Is Toxic," *San Antonio Express-News,* January 12, 2000.
29. Cadence Mertz, "Dirty War Continues—Illegal Dumpsite Found at Riverside," *Laredo Morning Times,* October 14, 1999.

30. Mount interview.
31. G.W. Levings et al., "Water Quality in the Rio Grande Valley, Colorado, New Mexico, and Texas, 1992–95," *U.S. Geological Survey Circular 1162*, May 18, 1998. http://water.usgs.gov.
32. Quoted in Souers, "Rio Grande Listed Among Nations' Most Endangered Rivers."
33. Rio Grande/Río Bravo Basin Coalition, "Santa Fe (Cochiti Reservoir) to Elephant Butte," April 2002. www.rioweb.org.
34. Quoted in Texas Public Employees for Environmental Responsibility, "Dumping on the Rio Grande." www.txpeer.org.
35. Quoted in Texas Public Employees for Environmental Responsibility, "Dumping on the Rio Grande."
36. Quoted in Texas Public Employees for Environmental Responsibility, "Dumping on the Rio Grande."
37. Stephen C. Saunders, "Endangered and Threatened Wildlife and Plants; Final Designation of Critical Habitat for the Rio Grande Silvery Minnow," U.S. Environmental Protection Agency, July 1999. www.epa.gov.
38. Quoted in Jan Reid, "The End of the River," *Texas Monthly,* January 2003, p. 48.
39. Quoted in Reid, "The End of the River," p. 48.

Chapter 5: Working Toward Water Security

40. Sandra Postel, *Last Oasis: Facing Water Scarcity.* New York: W.W. Norton, 1997, p. 185.
41. Souers, "Rio Grande Listed Among Nations' Most Endangered Rivers."
42. Bob Wiedenfeld, "Drip Irrigation to Replace Flood Irrigation," Texas Water Resources Institute. http://twri.tamu.edu.
43. Quoted in Bill Addington, "Challenging the Demand-Side of Water: Water and Sustainable Growth in the El Paso-Juárez Borderlands," *Resist,* vol., 9, no. 8, October 2002, p. 27.
44. Quoted in Addington, "Challenging the Demand-Side of Water," p. 27.
45. Quoted in Michael Malone et al., "Cadillac Desert: Water and the Transformation of Water," Public Broadcasting System, 1997. www.pbs.org.

46. David Ogden-Tamez, "Water: A Growing Concern in the Boarder's Desert Communities," New Mexico State University, May 1996. www.nmsu.edu.

47. Quoted in *Texas Water Savers,* "Harlingen Water Works Attracted Fruit of the Loom with Dependable Water Supply," vol. 4, no. 2, 1998, p. 76.

48. Ric Jensen, "Natural Wastewater Treatment System," *Texas Water Resources,* vol. 14, no. 2, Summer 1988, p. 96.

49. Quoted in Tania Soussan, "How Do You Stretch a River?" *Albuquerque Journal,* July 20, 2000.

50. Quoted in Soussan, "How Do You Stretch a River?"

51. Quoted in Susan Montoya Bryan, "In the West, Battle Rages Against the Invasive Salt Cedar," Environmental News Network, July 9, 2002. www.enn.com.

52. Quoted in Steve Taylor, "Water Dispute Called Biggest Bilateral Challenge," *Brownsville Herald,* June 21, 2002.

53. Quoted in Steve Taylor, "Secretary of State to Receive Note Saying Area Growers Don't Want Mexico's Water," *Valley Morning Star,* July, 15, 2002.

54. Ruben Navarrette Jr., "Water Wars Are Uneven," *Washington Post,* September 28, 2002.

Epilogue: A River Thirsting for Water

55. Rebecca Wodder, "Statement of President Rebecca R. Wodder," American Rivers, April 10, 2000. www.amrivers.org.

56. Postel, *Last Oasis,* p. 203.

For Further Reading

Laura Gilpin, *The Rio Grande River of Destiny*. New York: Duell, Sloan, and Pearce, 1949. Although an old book, this is one of the best books on the Rio Grande. Hundreds of black-and-white photographs of the river, geography, and the people living along the river are interspersed with excellent descriptive text and well-drawn maps.

Polly Schaafsma, *Rock Art in New Mexico*. Albuquerque: University of New Mexico Press, 1992. Comprehensive view of carvings and paintings on stone by Native Americans from 200 B.C. through the nineteenth century. Surveys the rock art of Utah, Arizona, New Mexico, northern Mexico, and West Texas, providing a visual record of Southwest Indian culture, religion, and society.

Armstrong Sperry, *Great River, Wide Land: The Rio Grande Through History*. New York: Macmillan, 1967. Provides a history of the Rio Grande and its peoples from the arrival of the Spanish through the Mexican-American War.

Jane Young, *Signs from the Ancestors: Zuni Cultural Symbolism and Perceptions of Rock Art*. Albuquerque: University of New Mexico Press, 1988. Provides many photographs and an interesting discussion on petroglyphs in the middle Rio Grande Valley.

Works Consulted

Books

Edwin Tappan Adney and Howard I. Chapelle, *The Bark Canoes and Skin Boats of North America.* Washington, DC: Museum of History and Technology, Smithsonian Institution, 1964. A detailed study of the bark canoes and skin boats of North American Indians that includes numerous photographs and drawings of various craft. Also discusses the history, materials, tools, design, and construction.

Scott A. Elias, *The Ice-Age History of Southwestern National Parks.* Washington, DC: Smithsonian Institution Press, 1977. A geologic history of the Southwest. Tracks the landscape changes made by natural phenomena and human settlement over the last ten thousand years.

Sandra Postel, *Last Oasis: Facing Water Scarcity.* New York: W.W. Norton, 1997. A landmark book that investigates the serious consequences of overusing and damaging many of the world's great rivers. Provides a long-term recommendation to correct past neglect.

Marc Reisner, *Cadillac Desert: The American West and Its Disappearing Water.* New York: Penguin Books, 1993. A history of how the West and Southwest supported a booming population and created economies dependent on the Colorado and Rio Grande Rivers. Discusses the great water projects and provides valuable insights into the politics of water and desert ecology.

David Roberts, *In Search of the Old Ones: Exploring the Anasazi World of the Southwest.* New York: Simon & Schuster, 1997. Chronicles the search for clues to the mystery of the Anasazi's abandonment of their extraordinary cliff dwellings some seven hundred years ago. Also discusses the arrival of the Spanish and their influence on Indian cultures along the Rio Grande.

Periodicals

Bill Addington, "Challenging the Demand-Side of Water: Water and Sustainable Growth in the El Paso–Juárez Borderlands," *Resist,* vol. 9, no. 8, October 2000.

Sherman R. Ellis et al., "Rio Grande Valley, Colorado, New Mexico, and Texas," *American Water Resources Association Bulletin,* vol. 29, no. 4, 1993.

Russell Gold, "Laredo Water Is Toxic," *San Antonio Express-News,* January 12, 2000.

Ric Jensen, "Natural Wastewater Treatment Systems," *Texas Water Resources,* vol. 14, no. 2, Summer 1988.

R.G. Mason, "Paleo-Maize Cultivation," *Southwestern Archaeology,* July 1999.

Reed McManus, "Way to Go: Rocks of Ages," *Sierra Club Magazine,* July/August 1966.

Cadence Mertz, "Dirty War Continues—Illegal Dumpsite Found at Riverside," *Laredo Morning Times,* October 14, 1999.

Ruben Navarrette Jr., "Water Wars Are Uneven," *Washington Post,* September 28, 2002.

James Pinkerton, "Blockage of Rio Grande's Flow to Gulf Could Have Harmful Effects, Some Fear," *Houston Chronicle,* May 12, 2001.

Jan Reid, "The End of the River," *Texas Monthly,* January 2003.

Rene Romo and Tania Soussan, "River Becomes Virtual Canal," *Albuquerque Journal,* July 19, 2000.

Bruce Selcraig, "The Great River Becomes a Great Sewer," *High Country News,* June 13, 1994.

Tania Soussan, "How Do You Stretch a River?" *Albuquerque Journal,* July 20, 2000.

———, "Sending Water on to Texas Is Challenge," *Albuquerque Journal,* July 16, 2000.

———, "Uses Battle for Middle Ground," *Albuquerque Journal,* July 18, 2000.

Steve Taylor, "Secretary of State to Receive Note Saying Area Growers Don't Want Mexico's Water," *Valley Morning Star,* July, 15, 2002.

———, "Water Dispute Called Biggest Bilateral Challenge," *Brownsville Herald,* June 21, 2002.

Texas Water Savers, "Harlingen Water Works Attracted Fruit of the Loom with Dependable Water Supply," vol. 4, no. 2, 1998.

Internet Sources

Wendell Barber, "Fish Kills Article for Windmill," Colorado River Municipal Water District. www.crmwd.org.

Big Bend National Park, "The Rio Grande: The Desert's Lifeblood," January 2003. www.nps.gov.

Susan Montoya Bryan, "In the West, Battle Rages Against the Invasive Salt Cedar," Environmental News Network, July 9, 2002. www.enn.com.

Karen Chapman, "Texas Center for Policy Studies/Dams on the Rio Grande," Texas Water Resources Institute, December 1998. http://twri.tamu.edu.

Linda Cordell, "Pueblo Indian Influence," City of Albuquerque, 1996. www.cabq.gov.

Forest Guardians, "Water and the Rio Grande," 2002. www.fguardians.org.

G.W. Levings et al., "Water Quality in the Rio Grande Valley, Colorado, New Mexico, and Texas, 1992–95," *U.S. Geological Survey Circular 1162*, May 18, 1998. www.water.usgs.gov.

Michael Malone et al., "Cadillac Desert: Water and the Trans-formation of Water," Public Broadcasting System, 1997. www.pbs.org.

New Mexico State Engineer Office, "Acequias," July 1997. www.seo.state.nm.us.

David Ogden-Tamez, "Water: A Growing Concern in the Border's Desert Communities," New Mexico State University, May 1996. www.nmsu.edu.

Rio Grande/Rio Bravo Basin Coalition, "Santa Fe (Cochiti Reservoir) to Elephant Butte," April 2002. www.rioweb.org.

———, "A Tour of the Rio Grande," February 2002. www.rioweb.org.

Stephen C. Saunders, "Endangered and Threatened Wildlife and Plants; Final Designation of Critical Habitat for the Rio Grande Silvery Minnow," U.S. Environment Protection Agency, July 1999, www.epa.gov.

Amy Souers, "Rio Grande Listed Among Nations' Most Endangered Rivers," American Rivers, April 10, 2000. www.amrivers.org.

Brian Tapley, "Rio Grande Delta Marshes," Center for Space Research, April 1999. www.csr.utexas.edu.

Texas Public Employees for Environmental Responsibility, "Dumping on the Rio Grande." www.txpeer.org.

Water in the West, "Rio Grande River Basin," 2002. www.waterinthe west.org.

Bob Wiedenfeld, "Drip Irrigation to Replace Flood Irrigation," Texas Water Resources Institute. www.twri.tamu.edu.

Rebecca Wodder, "Statement of President Rebecca R. Wodder," American Rivers, April 10, 2000. www.amrivers.org.

Websites

American Rivers (www.amrivers.org). A nonprofit conservation organization dedicated to protecting and restoring rivers nationwide. Provides numerous articles on the most endangered rivers in America, current and proposed river legislation, and recommendations for restoring the health of suffering rivers.

Big Bend National Park (www.nps.gov). Provides an array of information about the river, geology, and recreational offerings.

City of Albuquerque (www.cabq.gov). Provides information on Albuquerque's events, official city business, and tourism.

Environmental News Network (www.enn.com). Provides educational information about environmental issues throughout the world. Offers timely environmental news, live chats, interactive quizzes, daily feature stories, forums for debate, and a variety of audio and video programs.

Public Broadcasting System (www.pbs.org). Provides written articles and accompanying photographs covering hundreds of educational topics that are also presented on the PBS television station. An excellent and rich resource of pressing topics around the world.

Rio Grande/Río Bravo Basin Coalition (www.rioweb.org). A multinational, multicultural organization with leadership from the United States, Mexico, and the Pueblo nations. Its purpose is to help local communities restore and sustain the environment, their economies, and the social well-being of the Rio Grande/Río Bravo basin.

Texas Water Resources Institute (www.twri.tamu.edu). Serves as a focal point for water-related research at Texas universities to encourage discussions of statewide water issues through meetings and conferences. Provides information and links to educational information on critical water-program issues.

University of Kansas (www.ku.edu). Provides links and information on all university departments and events, including research of the Rio Grande.

University of New Mexico (www.unm.edu). Provides links and information on all university departments, events, and research.

U.S. Environmental Protection Agency (www.epa.gov). Provides online access to all Environmental Protection Agency documentation.

Water in the West (www.waterinthewest.org). A news and information service with a mission to develop an understanding of critical environmental issues in the western United States and Canada. Currently highlights the environmental, economic, social, and political status of ten major rivers, one of which is the Rio Grande.

Index

Picture Credits

About the Author

· ·

James Barter received his undergraduate degree in history and classics at the University of California at Berkeley, followed by graduate studies in ancient history and archaelogy at the University of Pennsylvania. Mr. Barter has taught history as well as Latin and Greek.

A Fulbright scholar at the American Academy in Rome, Mr. Barter worked on archaelogical sites in and around the city as well as on sites in the Naples area. Mr. Barter also has worked and traveled extensively in Greece.

Mr. Barter currently lives in Rancho Santa Fe, California, with his seventeen-year-old daughter, Kalista. She is a senior at Torrey Pines High School; works as a soccer referee; excels at math, physics, and English; and daily mulls her options for college next year. Mr. Barter's older daughter, Tiffany, lives nearby with her husband, Mike; teaches violin; and performs in classical music recitals.